The Millionaire's Roadmap

By Mark T. Lamkin, MBA, RFC

The Millionaire's Roadmap

By Mark T. Lamkin, MBA, RFC

Special Recognition

Thank you to my wife, Jennifer, my son, Zachary, and my daughter, Sydney, for understanding what it takes to build a successful practice.

Thank you to my mother, Diana, who has always been my biggest supporter and FAN!

Thank you to all my clients that have trusted me with their life decisions.

Thank you to the staff of Lamkin Wealth Managment for helping my dream become a reality.

Lamkin Wealth Management
5151 Jefferson Blvd., Ste. 100
Louisville, KY 40219

Office: (502) 961-6550 • Fax: (502) 961-6389

E-mail: mark.lamkin@lpl.com

www.marktlamkin.com

Providing world class "wealth-care" since 1991

Securities offered through Linsco Private Ledger
Member FINRA/SIPC and an Investment Advisor
Printed: September 2005

Table of Contents

The Millionaire's Roadmap

INTRODUCTION

Congratulations! If you are reading this book, then you are likely either retired or entering into retirement very shortly. For you, the hard part is over. If you are like many retirees in your age group, you have worked for 30-40 years, raised a family and perhaps, even fought in a war. You have faithfully served your family, community and country for decades and in short, you have earned a well-deserved rest.

With retirement, you have the opportunity to reap the fruits of your harvest. Retirement is play time; the time for you to finally take that cruise around the world or that cross-country trip in your new Prevost motor home. Or perhaps it's time to pursue your passion for writing, art, theatre, gardening, golf, you name it. My point.... now is your future and today is your time.

Even more, there has never been a better time to be retired. Despite the recent international turmoil, the world is relatively peaceful and America is as strong as ever. This is a great time to be an American and perhaps, an even better time to be a retired American.

In previous generations, retirement has been a time of isolation and loneliness. However, this will certainly not be the case for today's retirees. As a country, we are on the cusp of the great "baby boomer" retirement period. For the next 20 years, 10,000 people will turn 59 ½ each day. Therefore, not only do you finally have the time to "live the good life," but you will also have lots of company!

Another advantage possessed by today's retirees is the incredible progress in medical science. People are living longer than ever before. Just 100 years ago, the average life expectancy was just 45 years of age. Today, it has almost doubled to 85 years of age. And, ironically, as you get older, your life expectancy increases. For instance, a 59-year-old person has a life expectancy of an additional 26 years to age 85. However, a 69-year-old person has a life expectancy of an additional 18 years to age 87. And a 79-year-old person has a life expectancy of an additional 11 years to age 90. Therefore, there is a good chance that you will have plenty of time to do all of the things you've always wanted to do.

People are not only living longer lives but healthier lives as well. With medical advances and society's emphasis on healthier lifestyles, retirees are living more active lives. Many seniors are able to cycle, kayak and play tennis well into their 80s. In fact, in 1998, a 91-year-old man ran for the seventh time in the New York City Marathon. Amazingly, he recorded his best time in 1997 at the young age of 90.

The increasing longevity of retirees is changing perceptions about retirement. For instance, years ago, I heard a joke about a woman who had allowed her son to manage her finances for several years. On her 65th birthday, her son called to wish her a Happy Birthday. He excitedly told her, "Mom, I have some great news for you! Over the years, your investments have done very well. In fact, you have enough money to live comfortably until you are 100 years old!"

"And then what will I live on?" she replied.

Years ago, this may have seemed like an absurd question for the mother to ask but today, this seems like a valid question. In fact, according to U.S. census data, there are approximately 50,000 Americans who are 100 years old or more and that number is expected to double each decade. Therefore, in 40 years, there will be 800,000 Americans who are 100 years old or more. If you are 60 years old now and are in relatively good health, there is a decent chance that you will be one of them.

While this is certainly great news, from a financial standpoint it creates a challenge. Historically, many retirees have only effectively planned for the first 10 (or maybe 20) years of retirement. And this made sense when the average life expectancy was just 72 years of age. After all, who could have reasonably expected to live into their late 80s or 90s?

Without proper planning, some retirees will find themselves in the unenviable position of being forced back to work in their 70s, 80s or perhaps, even 90s. Sadly, these people will have to re-enter the workforce in an effort to earn enough money to make ends meet. And let's face it; no one wants to spend their golden years working at the golden arches. And while the door greeter job at Wal-Mart may be a really fun job, it will be a lot more fun for you if someone else is doing it.

Even some retirees who have adequately planned for a lengthy retirement will find themselves in this unenviable situation in their later years. The reason… because the proper investment strategies for retirement are fundamentally different from the investment strategies used in accumulation. Therefore, even people who have had great success at accumulating sizable retirement assets sometimes find it difficult to make the transfer from accumulation investing to retirement income investing. Quite simply, these are two very different types of investing.

By way of analogy, it's similar to the difference between climbing up a mountain and climbing down a mountain. In both cases, you will use many of the same tools. However, you will position those tools differently depending upon whether you are ascending or descending. The same is true in the investment context. Regardless of whether you are accumulating funds for retirement or managing those funds during retirement, you will use similar tools – stocks, bonds, cash equivalents, real estate, etc. However, during retirement, you must position yourself differently.

In fact, between the two types of investing – accumulation and distribution — it can be argued that retirement distribution investing is more challenging, just as climbing down a mountain is more dangerous than climbing up a mountain. During the climb up a mountain, you are usually full of energy and your goal is in front of you. However, during the descent, just the opposite is true. You are generally tired and you can not see your foot and hand holds because they are beneath you. And even worse, you have a greater distance to fall if you lose your grip. In a sense, the same is true with retirement investing.

Fortunately, in this book, you will learn strategies to keep you from "free falling" through retirement. These strategies can help you enjoy your golden years.

First, we will start by clarifying your goals, values and principles. Just as no two people have the same fingerprints, no two people should have the same Financial Life Plan. You will examine where you have been, where you are and where you are going. With a thorough understanding of your financial past, present and future, you can then begin to answer some of the fundamental questions necessary to help you develop your Financial Life Plan.

We will also review the fundamental components of a solid Financial Life Plan. By understanding the five building blocks of a Financial Life Plan, you will then be able to start creating a roadmap for your journey through retirement. In addition, we will discuss some of the most common mistakes investors make in an effort to help you steer clear of these common pitfalls. Finally, we will discuss the pros and cons of hiring a money manager and how to help make sure that you are hiring the right money manager to accomplish your goals (not theirs).

In short, by the end of this book, you will have learned the strategies necessary to allow you to be in the "driver's seat" with respect to your retirement. Now on to your roadmap.

— Chapter 1 —

THE ROAD AHEAD

Where Are You Going?

While all Americans dream of reaching that magical period of "retirement," the term has different meanings for different people. Some people view retirement as the time to sit on a beach with their spouse and just enjoy the sights and sounds of the tide rolling in. Others view retirement as the time to write the great American novel, backpack through Europe, or finally perfect their "short game" on the golf course. Some view retirement as the time to get more involved in civil, social, or religious organizations. Several "retirees" never fully retire from their profession but instead, see retirement as the opportunity to work part-time. And some of my happiest clients see retirement as a little bit of all of the above.

Of course, none of these definitions are wrong. Your retirement is precisely that — YOURS. You have every right to spend it as you see fit. The real question is how do *you* define "retirement?" Or better yet, have you defined what retirement will **mean for you**? Have you set goals for what you want to accomplish in your golden years? After all, the old adage is true: If you don't know where you're going, how can you possibly expect to get there? In fact, if you don't know where you're going, you won't even recognize "there" when you reach it.

Sadly, many people only have the vaguest notions of what they want out of retirement. In many cases, they get these notions from watching the retirement of their parents or friends. However, what worked for their parents or friends may not work for them.

For instance, there is a story of a man who was driving through the Black Hills near Mount Rushmore when he ran into a snowstorm. He soon lost all sense of direction but as luck would have it, he came behind a snow plow. Relieved, he kept as close to the snow plow as possible for what seemed like hours. Finally, the plow stopped and the driver came over to the man and asked, "Where are you headed?" The man replied, "I'm on my way to Montana." The snow plow driver laughed and said, "Well, you'll never get there following me. I'm plowing out this parking lot!"

From my experience, this is what often happens to many people who don't have a clear view of retirement. They end up following someone else who may be just going round and round in circles. That person may have a very valid reason for doing what he is doing. However, that reason may not be valid for you. Therefore, it's extremely important that you are clear on what ***your*** goals for retirement are.

Of course, chances are excellent that you already realize the importance of goal setting. After all, unless you just happened to hit the lottery in the last few years, your existing nest egg is probably the result of painstaking planning. For years, you saved and invested your money to prepare for this stage of your life. And quite simply, what has worked so well for you in the past is what will make your retirement successful – **planning** and **action**.

Moreover, goal setting is more than just a financial matter; it can actually be a matter of life and death. The simple truth is that people with passion and dreams actually live longer, healthier lives than those who are just going through the motions. According to some medical researchers, people who believe they have outlived their usefulness begin to experience apoptosis, or cell suicide. In essence, their cells begin to systemically separate from one another and die. Some researchers believe this happens because the brain sends a signal to the body that it is no longer needed, and the cells begin the process of deconstructing the body.

Furthermore, numerous studies have shown that people who stay active and involved in community and social activities live longer than those who don't. Perhaps, George Burns summed this up best when he said, "I can't die now – I'm booked." By being "booked," Burns was able to live until the age of 100. So stay "booked!"

Besides, let's face it, you still have a lot to contribute. Your skills, wisdom and experience are very much needed by the succeeding generations. Perhaps, this is why so many of the truly significant achievements throughout the years have been achieved by those over 60 years of age. In one study, researchers evaluated the lives of 400 famous people. They found that 35% of the things accomplished by these people were achieved while they were between the ages of 60 and 70. Another 23% of their accomplishments occurred between the ages of 70 and 80. And finally, 8% of accomplishments occurred after the age of 80. This means that 64%, or almost two-thirds, of their great works happened after the age of 60.

This research really begins to ring true when you consider the lives of people like Grandma Moses. As you probably know, Grandma Moses didn't start painting until she was 80 years old. However, in the remaining years of her life, she produced an astonishing 1,500 paintings. Perhaps, even more remarkable, 25% of the paintings were completed after her 100th birthday.

Or consider the case of Harland "Colonel" Sanders. At the age of 65, he began franchising his "secret blend of 11 herbs and spices" chicken recipe to restaurants across the country. In less than 10 years, he had signed up 600 restaurants to sell his chicken. A few years later, thousands of Kentucky Fried Chicken franchises were located in every state in the country and in many foreign countries as well. Today, there are more than 33,000 KFC restaurants in over 100 countries and it all started with a 65-year-old man with a chicken recipe, a dream, and a social security check.

I could spend the rest of this book relating story after story of men and women in 60s, 70s, and 80s and beyond who have done incredible things. The following are a few:

- George Bernard Shaw had one of his plays produced at the young age of 94 (two years later, he broke his leg when he fell out of a tree he was trimming in his backyard)
- Alfred Schweitzer was still performing operations in his hospital in Africa at the age of 89
- Michelangelo was 71 years old when he painted the Cistine chapel
- Winston Churchill was 65 years old when he assumed the role as Prime Minister of Great Britain (at 70, he gave his triumphant speech at D- Day)

Please don't misunderstand me here. I'm not suggesting that you must be the next Grandma Moses or Winston Churchill during your retirement. After all, this is *your* retirement and you are entitled to spend it any matter you choose. Instead, I am simply affirming what you already know, which is you still have a lot of living left to do. I makes sense for you to take a few minutes to get clear on exactly what you want to get out of the next 20, 30, or even 40 years of life.

If you've been retired for a few years now, you have probably been through this process in the past. You may have spent the last 10 or 20 years checking items off your wish list. Even still, it never hurts to take a fresh look at your current list of goals. We all change over time. Furthermore we often meet current goals. With the added insight of being successfully retired for a period of years, this is a great opportunity to fine-tune your goals for the future.

In the next few pages, I'm going to ask you to give some consideration to your physical life, your mental life, your family life, and the things you would like to experience. Going further, I want you to consider your ultimate legacy. If you are married, you may want to sit down with your spouse and give some collective thought to these questions so that the two of you share your goals together. In any event, I truly believe that answering the following questions will be a wise investment of your time.

Your Physical Life

What would you like to accomplish from a physical standpoint during your retirement? Would you like to get your golf handicap under 10? Or would you like to finally bowl a perfect game? Or perhaps, you would like to try something new, like surfing or scuba diving. Don't laugh! There are many senior citizens who are using their retirement years to do all of the physical activities that they could not do when they were chained to their office desks or apron strings while in their 20s, 30s, and 40s.

Below, please feel free to make a list of the sports or hobbies you would like to pursue during your retirement:

____

____

____

____

____

Your Mental Life

What intellectual pursuits would you like to engage in during your retirement? Would you like to go back to school and finally get your bachelor's or master's degree? Would you like to finally read all of the works of Shakespeare? Would you like to become the world's foremost authority on the New

Testament? The point is that retirement can be the time when you flex your intellectual muscle. After all, whatever you don't use, you lose, right?

Below, make a list of the intellectual pursuits you would like to engage in during your retirement:

____

____

____

____

____

Your Family Life

What is your dream for your relationship with your spouse, children, and grandchildren? Would you like to be able to finally take your spouse on that extended vacation that you've been promising for years? Or perhaps, you would like to just be able to take a walk together every afternoon. It's important to put your relationship goals on the "radar screen," so that you make sure to schedule in quality time with your loved ones along with your other activities.

This is particularly true with your relationships with your children, grandchildren and, dare I say, great grandchildren. Often times, your adult children move to other cities or states. Perhaps you move away to a home on the ocean or in the mountains. In any event, connecting with family members sometimes takes a little extra effort. In that case, it may become necessary to make a special goal to, visit your daughter in Arizona. Or you may wish to fly out the grandchildren for one week each summer. Whatever it is, you need to make special note of it. You have to have goals to achieve them.

Below, please to make a list of all the things you want to do with your spouse and family members during your retirement:

____

____

____

____

____

New Experiences

In my work with retirees and pre-retirees, I find that one of the most exciting aspects of retirement is the opportunity to do and see all of those things that they've been promising themselves they would do ***someday***. For many people, they become so used to putting their dreams off until someday, that they don't recognize someday when it arrives (hint – someday is now or very soon).

In J. Martin Kohe's book, *Your Greatest Power*, he tells a story of a man who went out in search of the touchstone. The touchstone was a small pebble with the power to turn any common metal into pure gold. The man knew that the touchstone was on the shores of the Black Sea, lying among millions of identical-looking pebbles. However, the touchstone was different because it was warm to the touch, while ordinary pebbles are cold.

Therefore, the man camped on the shore of the Black Sea and began testing pebbles by hand. All day, he walked up and down the beach testing stones. To prevent himself from testing the same stones over and over, whenever he encountered an ordinary pebble, he would toss it into the sea. For three years, he went up and down the shore, picking up pebbles, feeling them for warmth and tossing them into the sea. This was boring and tedious work but he knew that, *someday*, his efforts would pay off.

On the magical day, he picked up a pebble and to his surprise, it was warm to the touch. However, he instinctively threw it into the sea before his brain had a chance to register that this was the touchstone he had been searching for all along. Sadly, many people instinctively throw their "someday wishes" back into the ocean of life because they are so used to putting these experiences off. Don't let this happen to you.

What are some of the things that you've always dreamed of doing? Do you want to visit the Great Pyramids? Have you always wanted to own your own business? Many people are using their retirements to pursue the dream jobs that they couldn't pursue when they had the responsibility of raising a family. Or do you want to accomplish some goal that you've had on the "back burner?" Perhaps you want to get your book of poetry published or become a radio talk show host or grow the world's largest sweet potato. ***Well, someday is today***. As Nike would say, Just Do It!

Below, please feel free to make a list of all the new experiences you want to have during your retirement:

____

____

____

____

____

Your Legacy

Finally, you may want to give a little thought to what kind of legacy you will leave behind. Of course, there are several ways to leave a legacy. On the one hand, we leave a legacy with our service to others. What causes or organizations do you value? Would you like to volunteer your time and talents to further their causes? Would you like to donate (or increase your donations) to these organizations? Or perhaps, you would like to help send a grandchild or great grandchild to college.

On the other hand, we leave a legacy by the things we leave behind. Is there someone whom you would like to make sure is taken care of when you're gone? Or perhaps, you would like to endow a scholarship fund for your church, synagogue or temple. The point here is that these goals must be planned for in advance. But that isn't possible unless you get clear on them up front.

Below, please feel free to make a list of all the people, organizations and causes you would like to contribute to and how you would like to make that contribution.

____

____

____

____

____

— CHAPTER 2 —

THE ROAD BEHIND

Where Are You Coming From?

Now, that you've taken the time to set (or reset) your goals for retirement, you probably realize that you still have a lot more work (or rather "play") to do in life. There are probably many places you want to go, many things you want to see, and many people you want to meet. In this sense, your retirement can be seen as an extended vacation. Even when you are not traveling, you can still be enjoying yourself immensely. Of course, there is a lot of planning that goes into a successful vacation. And sadly, many people spend more time planning a one-week family vacation than they do planning a thirty-year retirement. You don't want to be one of these people. Vacations end quickly... your retirement shouldn't.

In this book, we are going to focus on how to fund your retirement "vacation." We are going to discuss strategies that hopefully will allow you to use your existing resources to take you everywhere you want to go. In the last chapter, we spent some time trying to get a clear picture on just that; where you want to go. Now, we will move on to the details of planning the actual trip.

However, before we can do that, we must first take into account one important thing about your retirement – YOU. Obviously, your retirement "itinerary" must take into account where *you* want to go. But it must also take into account where you currently are. For instance, if you we to call me on the phone and ask for directions to the Grand Ole Opry, I wouldn't have the first clue of what to tell you until you first answered this question: "Where are you?" Obviously, I can't tell you how to get from here to there if you don't know where "here" is.

The same thing applies to your journey through retirement. You must know where "here" is. **In financial terms, this means that you must take a complete assessment of your current resources**. How much have you accumulated in investments? How much income do you have coming in every month? How much will you incur in expenses each month? Answering these questions allows you to intelligently plan your itinerary.

Failing to get a clear picture of your current financial status is like leaving your home on a cross-country car trip without first counting the costs of gas, food, and lodging and just *hoping* that you have enough money for the trip. By doing so, you run a very real risk of running out of finances and becoming stranded out on the road. Moreover, even if you are lucky enough to make it back home, you will have virtually ruined your trip through constant worry about whether you will "get stuck in the middle of nowhere."

Surely, you don't want your retirement to be filled with such worry. Sadly, from my experience, many people are burdened by just this kind of anxiety throughout their retirement because they never get a clear picture of their current resources. These people generally fall into two camps.

The first camp consists of people who feel that they have so *much* money that they could never possibly run out of it. Unfortunately, sometimes this feeling is based more on fiction than fact. Retirement is almost always more expensive than you anticipate. I'm sure that if you've been retired for any length of time, you can attest to this fact. When you combine this fact with the fact that people are living longer than ever before, you can see how easy it is to overestimate the longevity of your resources. And even for those select few people who have accumulated more money than they could ever possibly spend in a lifetime, there is always the question of a legacy to consider. The only way to really determine whether you will be able to send your great grandchildren to college, fund scholarships at your church, or build a new arts center in your town is to take an accurate assessment of your current resources.

The second camp of people who do not fully assess their resources are those people who fear that they don't have enough resources for the trip. Therefore, rather than confronting what may be a painful reality, they figure that ignorance is bliss. However, the truth of the matter is that ignorance is not bliss; **ignorance is expensive**. And for people who may be already stretching their financial limits, ignorance is not an expense they can afford. This is particularly true because using the strategies we will discuss in this book, it may be possible to get a lot more "mileage" out of your existing assets.

Also, in addition, to your present financial picture, you need to take into account future events. Of course, none of us has a crystal ball into the future. Things will happen that are beyond our ability to foresee. For instance, no one could have predicted the tragedy of 9/11 and the effects it would have on our country. However, there are some future events that we can anticipate and these events should be part of our current financial picture. Are you expecting any sources of income in the near future (e.g., paid up life insurance premiums, vested stock options, inheritances, etc.)? Likewise, are you expecting any events that will decrease your current assets (e.g., education expenses for a family member, sizable gifts to family members or charities, etc.)? These likely events should be factored into any retirement planning calculations.

In addition to evaluating your current resources for your "journey," you must also take into account your "travel style." In other words, what values, principles and preferences are necessary for you to not only complete the journey but enjoy yourself in the process? This is a particularly important concern when you begin to choose investment "vehicles" to take you where you want to go.

As you know, investments differ in terms of security, volatility, risk, and potential rate of return. When choosing investments for retirement, you must take into account *your* comfort level with "riding" this type of vehicle. For instance, a motorcycle is probably the fastest and most fuel-efficient vehicle for highway travel. But would you really feel comfortable riding one on a cross-country trip? If you are like most people, the answer is "no." The same is true with investments. There are some investments that historically have delivered higher rates of returns than their counterparts. However, when evaluating the best investment for you, the potential rate of return is just one of many factors. The most important factor should be your comfort level with the risks associated with that investment. After all, your retirement is going to be far less enjoyable if you are holding on for dear life and constantly worrying about financial disaster.

In determining your comfort level, perhaps the most important thing is to evaluate your past "travel style." How did you accumulate what you have today? Was it through fixed-rate investments like CDs, treasury bonds, and municipal bonds? Or did you accumulate your current assets in growth investments like mutual funds, individual stocks, and real estate? Did the bulk of your assets come in some other manner, such as through the sale of your business, the vesting of stock options in your employer, the maturity of your pension fund, or an inheritance?

Another feature of your travel style is not just the "vehicles" you've traveled in but how you traveled in them. In other words, are you more comfortable as a driver or a passenger? For instance, if you accumulated funds through stock appreciation, did you pick the stocks yourself or did you rely on the advice of a broker, mutual fund manager, or financial advisor? What lessons did you learn about investing in this manner? What worked well for you? What didn't work so well? How will you feel most comfortable "traveling" through your retirement?

The last thing to consider is your values and principles. You've spent a lifetime living your life by certain principles. Surely, retirement is not the time to abandon the principles that have served you so well for your entire life. Some of these principles are financially-based principles. For instance, if you've lived by a rule that you would never borrow funds to make investments, then retirement is not the time to start buying technology stocks on margin. Please note that while the strategies presented in this book may require you to change your approach on some aspects of your financial life, they will not require you to forsake the fundamental investment principles that have gotten you this far in the first place. If it ain't broken, don't fix it.

In addition to holding firm to your financial principles, you will certainly want to remain faithful to your moral principles. For instance, if you have always refused to invest in companies in certain industries or in companies that are active in causes contrary to your values, then your retirement investments should reflect the same values. This is the case even if these companies become the "hot" investments of the 21st century. This may sound strange coming from a financial advisor but there are some things more important than money. Your values and principles are two of these things. As it says in the Bible, "What shall it profit a man if he shall gain the whole world and lose his own soul!"

By first giving careful consideration to your current location, your travel style and your values and principles, you will be much better prepared to begin the process of creating a detailed roadmap to take you through your retirement journey. In the next chapter, we will discuss precisely how to do just that. Also, you will be introduced to the five building blocks of a Financial Life Plan.

Summary

By this point of the book you should have:

1. Defined how you would like your retirement to look ... include specific goals that you would like to achieve.
2. Taken a complete financial inventory of your assets.
3. Taken time to understand how you have accumulated what you have.
4. Began to develop your monthly spending budget.
5. Began thinking about your new lifestyle and if that lifestyle includes work.

— CHAPTER 3 —

CREATING A ROADMAP

Connecting the Dots

Now, that you know where you are and where you want to go, creating your retirement roadmap is as simple as connecting the dots. The important thing about retirement planning is to work with the end in mind. Your end (or goal) should be to have enough monthly income to live your ideal retirement lifestyle and enough remaining assets to leave behind to your children, your grand children, and your favorite causes.

Therefore, the first step in this process is to determine your monthly budget during retirement. Historically, financial planners have used the 70% rule. In other words, they estimated that the typical retiree could live off just 70% of their income at the time of retirement. The reasoning behind this rule was that certain expenses decrease during retirement. For instance, automobile expenses related to commuting (e.g., gasoline, wear and tear, etc.) are reduced dramatically during retirement. The same is true for other work-related expenses, such as clothing and meals at restaurants.

However, this rule oversimplifies the process. The truth of the matter is that you are not the "typical" retiree. In fact, no

Figure 3.1

MONTHLY EXPENSES	
Mortgage or Rent	$__________
Home Repairs	$__________
Maintenance/Gardening/Housekeeping	$__________
Utilities (Gas/Water/Electric/Trash)	$__________
Cable TV	$__________
Telephone	$__________
Car Payments	$__________
Gasoline/Oil	$__________
Auto Repairs/Maintenance	$__________
Groceries	$__________
Toiletries/Household Products	$__________
Homeowner's/Renter's Insurance	$__________
Automobile Insurance	$__________
Medical/Dental Insurance	$__________
Life Insurance	$__________
Entertainment/Recreation	$__________
Travel (Airfare, cruises, lodging)	$__________
Eating out	$__________
Clothing	$__________
Hobbies	$__________
Newspapers/Magazines	$__________
Computer/Internet Expense	$__________
Gifts/Donations	$__________
Clubs/Associations	$__________
Federal Income Tax	$__________
State Income Tax	$__________
Local Property Tax	$__________
Excise Taxes (car, other personal property)	$__________
Miscellaneous (pets, tuition, etc.)	$__________
TOTAL EXPENSES	**$__________**

one is a typical retiree. We all have different goals and aspirations for our retirement years. For some people, the cost of living will decrease by more than 70%. For others, the cost of living will decrease less. In fact, for some retirees, the cost of living will increase as they travel, enroll in college, start a business or lend greater support to a favorite charity. For this reason, it's important for each person to calculate their own budget during retirement. It's likely that you've already constructed such a budget, but if not, a sample worksheet is provided **Figure 3.1**.

The second step is to then calculate your income during your retirement years. For many people, this is much easier than calculating expenses because the sources of income are fewer. They can be grouped into the general categories listed in **Figure 3.2**.

Figure 3.2

MONTHLY INCOME	
Salary/Wages/Tips	$__________
Business Income	$__________
Pension Income	$__________
Social Security Income	$__________
Interest Income	$__________
Capital Gains	$__________
Dividends	$__________
Property Rental Income	$__________
TOTAL INCOME	**$**__________

Once you've taken stock of your income and expenses, then you have a much clearer picture of the road ahead. For instance, if you discover that your expenses exceed your income, then you can make one of three adjustments: (1) you can scale back your retirement lifestyle, (2) you can go back to work part-time to earn additional income; or (3) you can seek to make your money work harder for you. Obviously, for most people, the third option is the most attractive. It's for this reason that I've written this book. In the coming chapters, we're going to explore ways to develop a sound Financial Life Plan and strategies designed to help you do just that.

Of course, some of you find yourselves in the advantageous position of having more income than expenses. Even if this is the case, you aren't out of the woods yet. You must still deal with a huge obstacle – inflation. Over time, inflation can turn your nest egg into chicken feed. For instance, let's take the case of Ralph and Rita Retiree. They retire at the age of 55 with a nest egg of $1,000,000. Furthermore, they calculate their monthly expenses to be just $4,000, while their monthly income is $5,000. Therefore, during their first year of retirement, they are actually growing their nest egg. It seems as if Ralph and Rita have it made. They will never run out of money, right?

If it were not for the potentially devastating effects of inflation, this would be true. But inflation has a strange way of turning a dollar saved into a quarter earned. After all, think back to 40 years ago. If you are like many people, your monthly income now is more than your *annual* income back then. Part of this dramatic increase in your income can be attributed to inflation. So just think about the next forty years and how much your income will have to grow to keep up with inflation. How much was a postage stamp 20 years ago? How much was a new car in the 1960's? Inflation is real.

To illustrate, let's go back to the example of Ralph and Rita. Let's assume that inflation remains at its historically low rate of just 3%. Or let's further assume that Ralph's and Rita's income from social security, pensions, and investments remains constant. As you remember, in the first year of retirement, Ralph and Rita are actually making an extra $12,000 a year. However, by age 65, their expenditures are now slightly more than $5,000 per month and they start to nibble away a little bit at their nest egg. By age 75, their expenditures are now more than $7,000 per month and they are reducing their next age by $25,000 per year. By age 85, their monthly expenditures are now almost $10,000 and they are reducing their next egg at the rate of more than $50,000 per year. At age 93, when their monthly expenditures hit $12,000, they will run out of money.

Of course, Ralph and Rita retired in better financial shape than most. Therefore, if inflation could eat away their life savings so effectively, just imagine the havoc it can wreak on most retirees. For this reason, a sound Financial Life Plan (FLP) is an absolute necessity for most retirees. An FLP strives to do two things: (1) it seeks to decrease expenses (without reducing lifestyle) and (2) it seeks to increase income. When done correctly, these strategies can more than offset the effects of inflation.

The five fundamental building blocks of a sound Financial Life Plan are:

1. Sound investments
2. Retirement distribution strategies
3. Income tax reduction strategies
4. Long-term care planning
5. Dignity and estate planning

Sound Investments

One way to try to offset the ravages of inflation is to make sound investments that have the potential to keep up with (or preferably, outpace) inflation. While this may seem obvious, it is harder said than done and certainly, more difficult during retirement than during the accumulation years. During the accumulation years, you had the luxury of time and an alternative source of income. You were not as concerned about the short-term fluctuations in the market because you were investing for 20, 30, or 40 years into the future. However, during retirement this perspective changes. Furthermore, during retirement, you may need to draw income from your investments, which was likely not the case during the accumulation years.

Therefore, choosing sound investments during retirement involves an added layer of complexity. However, it can be done. In the next two chapters, we'll discuss some of the basics of investing. Furthermore, we'll discuss four habits of wealthy investors and five of the most common mistakes of investing. Lastly, we'll discuss some particular investment vehicles that can turn into "lemons."

Retirement Distribution Strategies

For many retirees, some of the most puzzling questions involve distributions from retirement accounts; namely "When do I start withdrawing funds from my accounts and how much should I withdraw?" Needless to say, the answers to these questions will vary widely from person to person. Furthermore, the answers can have a significant impact on your financial future.

For one, no one wants to start withdrawing funds too early and find themselves with too much retirement at the end of the money. Second, in most cases, withdrawals from retirement accounts have tax consequences; sometimes, severe consequences. As we discussed earlier, one of the ways to stave off inflation is to reduce expenses. Therefore, to the extent you can reduce your tax burden, you increase your changes of staying ahead of inflation.

Tax Reduction Strategies

If you're like most Americans, then throughout your entire lifetime, your single biggest expense has been taxes. You've paid federal income taxes, state income taxes, social security taxes, excise taxes, property taxes, sales taxes, you name it. You have spent more of your hard-earned money on taxes than you did on your home, the education of your children, or any other single expenditure.

Unfortunately, you're not done paying taxes yet. However, you can significantly reduce the taxes you will pay as a retiree. This is especially crucial during retirement years because your ability to affect the other half of the equation (income) may be limited. For instance, during your working years, if you experienced an increase in expenses, then you could work more overtime at your job or even get a second job to even out your cash flow. This may not be possible during your retirement years, and even if possible, it wouldn't be preferable. For this reason, getting your tax situation under control is even more crucial during this period of life.

In addition, reducing your tax burden will reduce your overall level of expenses and help you in the battle against inflation. In fact, cutting your tax bill is one of the best ways to reduce expenses because it doesn't require you to scale back your retirement lifestyle. For many retirees, if the choice is between cutting out a cruise to the Bahamas or cutting out excess taxes, the choice is easy to make.

Therefore, in future chapters, we will discuss the tax consequences of various investments with an eye towards greatly reducing your tax burden. In many cases, the goal won't be so much to avoid taxes but rather to simply defer them. As you probably know, there is a tremendous financial benefit that comes from deferring the payment of taxes as long as possible. I tell investors frequently, to be a successful investor you need to defer death and taxes as long as possible.

Long-Term Care Planning

Interestingly, the greatest financial risk facing many retirees is not the stock market or our current geopolitical turmoil. Instead, it's the astronomical cost of long-term care. This can be defined as home health care, assisted living, or nursing home care. In many areas of the country, nursing home care can cost $75,000 or more per *year*. Even more, the average nursing home stay is about three years and some patients stay in nursing homes for double or triple that length of time.

As you can imagine, the need for a lengthy nursing home stay (or assisted living arrangement) can throw any Financial Life Plan into a tailspin. Many retirees wind up spending all of their resources on these types of arrangements, leaving nothing for their children and grand children. Therefore, no sound FLP can neglect long-term care planning, whether through the purchase of long-term care insurance or by using other strategies, when insurance is either unavailable or cost prohibitive. Planning is critical. Do you have a goal of being a ward of the state? Do you like the idea of bankrupting your spouse? Scary but true. We all need to plan for the expense of long term care.

Dignity and Estate Planning

The final building block of a sound FLP involves dignity planning and estate planning. In dignity planning, the goal involves allowing you to keep your dignity intact during the entire span of your lifetime. Right up to the very end when you might not be in a position to make decisions for yourself. Therefore, dignity planning usually involves the drafting and execution of a living will. In this document, you state your wishes about medical care that you'd like to receive (or not receive) in certain dire situations. Another common dignity document is a health care power of attorney, which appoints a person of your choosing to make decisions for you if you become incapacitated. In some cases, you will want to execute a more general power of attorney that gives this person or another individual the right to act on your behalf in financial matters as well.

Proper estate planning allows you to pass on your property in accordance with your wishes. In fact, unless some level of estate planning is done, it's almost a certainty that your wishes will not be carried out upon your death. Without a will, the state gets to decide the division of your assets; not you. Second, even if you have a will, estate taxes may prevent your loved ones from honoring your wishes.

For instance, we've all read about the families of farmers or small businesspeople who had to sell the family farm or the family business just to pay federal estate taxes. In these cases, the IRS defeated the intent of people who worked an entire lifetime to build a legacy to pass down to their children. This is tragic, and perhaps all the more so because in some cases, it was preventable.

There are a number of strategies you can use to reduce estate taxes. And even when they must be paid, it may be possible to use other investments to keep your farm, business, home, or other important asset intact for future generations.

Notes

— CHAPTER 4 —

CHOOSING YOUR INVESTMENT VEHICLES

Four Habits Of Wealthy Retirement Investors

Of course, if you've reached the point of accumulating significant retirement assets, you're already familiar with the basics of investing. However, as previously stated, retirement investing is fundamentally different from accumulation investing. Let's discuss four habits of wealthy retirement investors:

1 Set Specific Measurable Goals

2. Time Not Timing

3. Understanding and Taking Prudent Risks

4. Asset Allocation and Diversification

Habit #1: Set Specific Measurable Goals

As we've discussed before, how can you get to where you want to go if you don't know where you want to go? Of course, even when you've established a destination, you must set specific and measurable goals to accurately monitor your progress.

For instance, let's suppose you live in New York and you plan to drive to California to attend a wedding there in five days. In this case, you would likely set mini-goals along the way to make sure that you were on schedule to arrive in California on time. You might set a goal of reaching the Ohio by the end of the first day and the Mississippi River by the end of the second day and so on. You would definitely want to have some indication of how much progress you were making.

This way, if you get off track, you can make appropriate adjustments. Let's suppose that you've planned several stops along your route to California. If you notice that you are off-schedule, then you can cut out one or two of those stops to make up for lost time. You may decide to just drive through Las Vegas and instead, stop there on your return trip.

The same principle applies to your financial trip through retirement. Using the principles discussed in earlier chapters, you may have established some goals as far as your required annual rate of return. It's important that this goal be specific (and preferably conservative). In this manner, if you find that you are falling short of this goal, you can make adequate adjustments to your portfolio. The same is true on the other side of the coin. If you notice that your investments are doing better than expected for a sustained period of time, you may want to take that opportunity to recalculate your required rate of return and shift some of your assets to other, more conservative investments.

Once again, all of this is only possible if you know where you're going (i.e., you've set specific measurable goals) and you monitor your progress along the way.

Habit #2: Time not Timing

The fundamental maxim for sound investing is to buy low and sell high. Given this, it's tempting to attempt to time the market. Or, in other words, to try to buy into the market at its low points and sell out of the market at its high points. The problem with this strategy is that it's nearly impossible to determine *beforehand* these highs and lows. As of this writing, no one has yet to develop a method to predetermine these highs and lows and I expect that no one ever will. I have worked with many investors that have tried it….most have actually lost money.

Therefore, the focus should not be on **timing** but **time**. Over time, the stock market has provided better returns than most other types of investment. However, those returns were based on staying invested in the market. For instance, if you had invested in the S&P from December 31, 1987 through December 31, 1997, you would have earned an annualized total return of **18.05%** for that 10-year period. However, if you jumped in and out of the market and managed to miss just the best 10 trading days of that period, your return would have only been 14.26%. And if you missed the best 40 days, your return would have been a paltry 6.91%. (Past performance is no guarantee of future results. The S&P 500 is an unmanaged index which cannot be invested into directly.)

Figure 4.1

The S&P 500 (12/31/87-12/31/97)

	Annualized total return
Fully Invested	18.05%
Missed best 10 days	14.26%
Missed best 20 days	11.46%
Missed best 30 days	9.06%
Missed best 40 days	6.91%

Therefore, most experts agree that one key when seeking to maximize your stock market returns is to *stay* invested. For many people, the hard part isn't staying invested but getting invested in the first place. Some would be investors are never able to get into the game. They are stuck on the sidelines waiting for the market to finally "bottom out." After all, there is always some event that makes "later" seem like a better time to invest in the market. For instance, after the bombing of Pearl Harbor in 1941, it must have seemed like a terrible time to invest. The same could be said for the outbreak of the Korean War, the assassination of President Kennedy, the escalation of the Vietnam conflict, the Watergate scandal, the recession of the early 1980s, the S&L debacle, the stock market crash of 1987, the Persian Gulf War, and of course, the awful events of September 11, 2001.

However, as of this writing, the Dow Jones Industrial Average (an unmanaged index which cannot be invested into directly) is up more than 9,400% since the bombing of Pearl Harbor. Likewise, it's up almost 1,500% since the assassination of President Kennedy. The Dow is up more than 500% since the stock market crash of 1987. In fact, as of this writing the market is up almost 10% since 9/11 (past performance is no guarantee of future results). The market appears to be resilient as it has bounced back time and time again after adversity.

Of course, catastrophic events aren't the only causes of market downturns. Investing in securities involves risks, including possible loss of principal. According to some analysts, periodically, the market "corrects" itself when prices get out of hand. Here is an excerpt from an article in a popular magazine explaining one correction.

> *"To the question, 'What has gone wrong in the stock market?' There can only be one real answer: the market came down because it had gone too high. It fell precipitously, and for some people ruinously, because so many stocks had so far to fall before they would reach any firm and solid foundation. It was such a vast bull market,*

> *rising so spectacularly, that anybody with eyes was bound to see it. And anyone with a normal quota of human greed was bound to hanker to climb aboard.... There were new companies with untried management, small earnings and dubious prospects – with nothing but a prayer and a catchy space age name which are bid up as much as 400% within a few months. From time to time some of the experts had their doubt.... But the investors kept pouring in and anybody who wanted to have money in the market had to ride along with their optimism."*

You might think that this excerpt was taken from a recent issue of Forbes or Fortune. Yet, it comes from an article written in the summer issue of *LIFE* magazine in **1962**. As you can see, the more things change, the more they stay the same.

Habit #3: Understanding and Taking Prudent Risks

Of course, even with the usually rosy long-term outlook of the market, there are many risks to investing in stocks. Understanding these risks, and taking prudent measures to minimize them, is important to all investors. However, it's critical to retirement investors. After all, if you lose your life savings in the stock market at age 30, it's regrettable but more than likely fixable. On the other hand, if you lose your life savings in the market at age 80, it's a tragedy.

Principal Risk

One of the risks faced by all stock investors is principal risk – the risk you will lose some or all of your principal investment. Facing this risk as a retiree can be particularly taxing. After all, not only do you lose your principal investment but also the ability to earn money from that principal. If you depend upon such income to meet your expenses during retirement, then this can be devastating.

This risk can't be altogether eliminated when investing in stocks. When you purchase shares of IBM or AT&T for example, you take a stake in the company. If the company goes bankrupt, then your stake will be worth little or nothing. Likewise, if the value of the company drops in the eyes of the investment company, you won't be able to sell your shares at the price you paid for them. As a result, you can lose some or all of your principal.

One way to seek to protect against this risk is to limit your investments to stable companies with a good track record of earnings. Of course, this strategy won't eliminate your principal risk since even the largest companies suffer declines and even bankruptcies, such as Enron, K-Mart, WorldCom, etc. For this reason, it's imperative to diversify your holdings among many stocks. The rationale here is that while you may lose principal in some investments, you potentially have principal gains in other investments to help offset losses. However, diversification does not ensure success nor guarantee against loss in periods of declining markets and does not eliminate principal risk. It's simply part of the territory when you invest in stocks.

Interest Rate Risk

Another risk of investing in stocks is interest rate risk. As a general rule, the stock market moves in an inverse correlation to the movement of interest rates. Or in other words, when interest rates fall, stock prices go up and vice versa. Of course, this correlation isn't exact. Even when interest rates are rising sharply, many stocks are rising as well. Likewise, even when interest rates fall, many stocks decline. Nevertheless, overall, interest rates and stock prices tend to move in opposite directions.

The reason for this is simply a product of supply and demand. When interest rates increase, investors begin to shift more of their money to interest-bearing investments, which often entail less principal risk. This shift creates more sellers and fewer buyers of stock, depressing prices. The opposite phenomenon occurs when interest rates fall. Investors begin to shift their resources to the stock market in search of higher returns. This shift creates more buyers and fewer sellers, increasing stock prices.

Of course, with the possible exception of Alan Greenspan, no one has a crystal ball that can accurately predict the direction of interest rates. Nevertheless, understanding interest rate risk can help you to reduce your risk of principal loss if you spot a trend of ever-increasing interest rates.

Market Risk

Another risk for stock investors is market risk. As you know, the stock market is in a constant state of flux. Each trading day, companies rise and fall in value, sometimes to the tune of billions of dollars, and for no apparent reason. One day, a company's stock may rise 5% and the next day, it may fall 10%. This can happen even in the absence of any news or developments that would affect the company's future profitability. The stock market is simply fickle.

Therefore, at any time, there is a very real risk that the value of your shares will mysteriously drop. This is the case even for companies with incredible prospects. For instance, let's take the case of Microsoft. During the 1980s and 1990s, this company produced astronomical returns for its investors. For instance, a $10,000 investment in Microsoft in 1986 would have been valued at more than $4,721,000 just 17 years later in 2003.[i] However, Microsoft's stock price didn't just shoot straight up over that time period. There were many

Figure 4.2

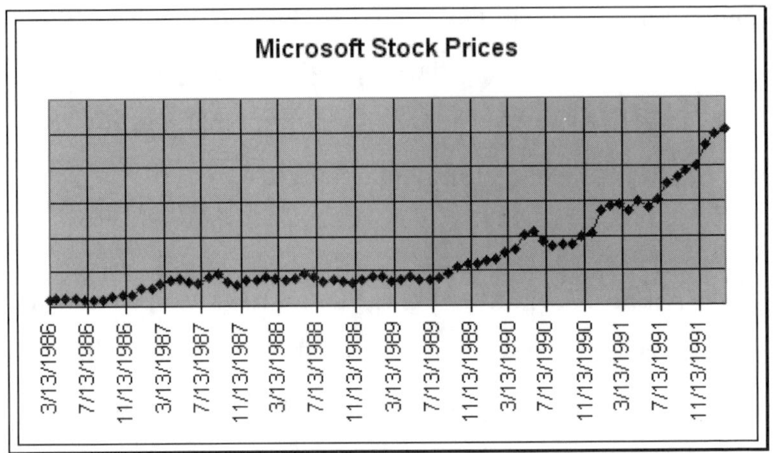

peaks and valleys. For instance, the chart below illustrates the ascent of Microsoft's stock value from 1986 to 1992.

During its first six years as a public company, Microsoft's value increased *28* fold. Yet, as you can see, the progression wasn't linear. There were many months when the value of the stock fell. This same kind of volatility can be seen in the market as a whole. During accumulation mode, this market risk is a little more tolerable because you had the advantage of time on your side. You had time to ride out a down period for the opportunity for future upswings. However, this isn't the case during retirement when you may be depending upon part of the principal increase to fund your retirement lifestyle.

For instance, from 1934 to 2002, the average rate of return for the S&P 500 was approximately 11%. If the stock market rose 11% each and every year, then a retiree could use this return to finance part of his or her retirement lifestyle. A retiree could simply sell some of the appreciated shares each year.

For instance, let's suppose you have $300,000 in an S&P index fund. Historically, such a fund has earned you a rate of return of 11%. You currently need $2,000 per month to fund your retirement lifestyle. If you could count on receiving 11% in stock appreciation each year, you would earn $33,000 in annual appreciation. *Theoretically*, each year, you could sell $24,000 worth of stock and still watch your nest egg grow. In fact, after 10 years and assuming a modest rate of inflation of 3%, you'd not only have all of your principal but you'd have an additional $103,175 ($403,175 in total).

Figure 4.3

Year	Annual Expenditures	Nest Egg Blance
1	$24,000.00	$309,000.00
2	$24,720.00	$318,270.00
3	$25,461.60	$327,818.10
4	$26,225.45	$337,652.64
5	$27,012.21	$347,782.22
6	$27,822.58	$358,215.69
7	$28,657.26	$368,962.16
8	$29,516.97	$380,031.02
9	$30,402.48	$391,431.96
10	$31,314.56	$403,174.91

Of course, we all know that stock market returns aren't uniform. During the 68 years between 1934 and 2002, the S&P didn't increase 11% each year. Some years, the return was well above 11% and other years, the return was well below 11%. In fact, during some years, the S&P actually lost ground.

So let's assume that instead of earning 11% each year, you earn 27% the first year but you lose 5% the next year and so on. Your overall return would be close to 11%. However, because of your need to annually withdraw money (even when you aren't earning any), you'd accumulate$32,000 less than if your return was stable.

Figure 4.4

Year	Annual Expenditures	Nest Egg Blance
1	$24,000.00	$357,000.00
2	$24,720.00	$314,430.00
3	$25,461.60	$373,864.50
4	$26,225.45	$328,945.83
5	$27,012.21	$390,748.99
6	$27,822.58	$343,388.96
7	$28,657.26	$407,446.73
8	$29,516.97	$357,557.42
9	$30,402.48	$423,695.44
10	$31,314.56	$371,196.11

Of course, this isn't much of a problem provided that your good years precede your bad years and the bad years don't decline by a greater percentage than the good years. In other words, so long as you make money first and then lose some of it back the next year. However, if the opposite is true, then you could be in real trouble. For instance, let's suppose you lose 5% in the first year and gain 27% the next year and this pattern continues. After 10 years, you'll only have a little more than you started with at $307,239. Even worse, in 25 years, you'll run out of money. For this reason, market risk is a major risk to manage, even when stock investments are performing well. (See **Figure 4.5**)

Political Risk

Another form of risk associated with stocks is political risk. Changes in the law can negatively impact the prospects of the company in which you've invested. For instance, if Congress were to pass a law banning the sale of cigarettes, this law would have a devastating effect on the stock price of Philip Morris and other tobacco companies.

And political risk is most pronounced when you invest in foreign stocks, particularly those of companies located in third world countries. Often, when a third world government is overthrown, many business interests are nationalized, leaving the stock holders holding worthless certificates.

Figure 4.5

Year	Annual Expenditures	Nest Egg Blance
1	$24,000.00	$ 261,000.00
2	$24,720.00	$ 306,750.00
3	$25,461.60	$ 265,950.90
4	$26,225.45	$ 311,532.20
5	$27,012.21	$ 268,943.37
6	$27,822.58	$ 313,735.51
7	$28,657.26	$ 269,391.48
8	$29,516.97	$ 312,610.20
9	$30,402.48	$ 266,577.21
10	$31,314.56	$ 307,238.50
11	$32,253.99	$ 259,622.58
12	$33,221.61	$ 296,499.07
13	$34,218.26	$ 247,455.85
14	$35,244.81	$ 279,024.12
15	$36,302.15	$ 228,770.76
16	$37,391.22	$ 253,147.65
17	$38,512.95	$ 201,977.31
18	$39,668.34	$ 216,842.85
19	$40,858.39	$ 165,142.31
20	$42,084.15	$ 167,646.59
21	$43,346.67	$ 115,917.59
22	$44,647.07	$ 102,568.27
23	$45,986.48	$ 51,453.37
24	$47,366.08	$ 17,979.71
25	$48,787.06	*OUT OF MONEY*

FIXED INCOME INVESTMENTS

Due to risks of owning stocks, many retirees prefer to invest a large percentage of their assets in "safer" fixed income investments, like bonds, notes and bills. However, as you will see, these investments carry their own significant risks.

Credit Risk

Credit risk is a form of principal risk that occurs when the issuer of the debt security is unable to repay the loan. While the debt obligations of the federal government are backed by the full faith and credit of the U.S. government (i.e., if there's not enough money in the Treasury, they can always print more of it), the same thing can't be said for corporate and municipal bonds. Corporations and municipal governments can (and do) go bankrupt. When this happens, bond holders will lose some of their principal. However, bond holders will fare much better than stock holders, who usually lose all (or almost all) of their principal.

Interest Rate Risk

Perhaps the greatest risk for fixed income investors is interest rate risk. This is also perhaps the most misunderstood and overlooked risk for these investors. When interest rates rise, this would seem to be a good thing for fixed income investors. For instance, if interest rates go from 4% to 8%, fixed income investors would receive double the income, right? Well, not necessarily.

For instance, let's suppose you invested $100,000 last year in a 30-year U.S. Treasury bond yielding interest at the rate of 5%. Therefore, each year, you receive $5,000 in interest on this bond. Let's suppose that this year interest rates rise sharply so that the new 30-year Treasury bonds pay an interest rate of 8%. You begin to think that if you could move your money to the new bonds, you could earn an additional $3,000 per year in interest. However, this simply isn't the case.

For you to move your funds to the new bonds, you will have to find a buyer for your old bonds. However, no one will be willing to pay you full price for 5% bonds when they can buy 8% from the federal government. As a result, the only way to sell those bonds will be to offer them at a discount so that the new buyer is also receiving an interest rate of 8%. Therefore, to sell your bonds, you will have to offer them at a price close to $62,500.

Of course, this wouldn't do you any good because when you invested this lower amount in the new bonds, you would only receive annual interest payments of approximately $5,000; the same amount you were earning before. Even worse, you would have traded away over $37,000 in principal to get the same return. Therefore, for all practical purposes, once you buy a fixed income security, you are stuck with that interest rate until it secures.

This can be a real problem if you need to get access to your principal at some point before the term expires. For instance, given the above example, let's suppose you find yourself in a position where you need access to $50,000 in cash. To raise this amount of money, you have to sell almost $80,000 worth of bonds, leaving you with just $20,000, earning a mere $1,000 per year in interest.

Most financial professionals suggest that retirees "ladder" the maturity of their bonds. As 30-year bonds have the highest yields, it's tempting for retirees to put their money to work at these higher rates. However, due to the interest rate risk inherent in all bonds, a better strategy is to spread your investments out over bonds with various maturities. For instance, you could take that same $100,000 and split it between 1-year, 2-year, 5-year, 10-year and 30-year bonds. Sure, your total rate of return would be lower today but it would allow you to take advantage of possible higher future interest rates when your bonds mature. Furthermore, should you ever need to withdraw some funds; you won't have to pay such a hefty price in terms of depreciation.

Of course, it should be noted that there is an opposite side of the coin – the situation where interest rates fall sharply. In this case, your bonds become even more valuable and you are able to sell them at a profit. Of course, as of this writing, interest rates are at a 30-year low and the prospects of them falling much further are slim. Furthermore, gambling on the future direction of interest rates seems to defeat the purpose of investing in the "safety" of fixed income securities.

Inflation Risk

As we discussed in the last chapter, inflation is one of the greatest risks faced by retirees. And while inflation lessens the real rate of return for all investments, it wreaks particular havoc on fixed income returns. For one, most fixed income investments simply return the investor's principal after some period of time. However, due to inflation, the returned principal buys less than it did when originally invested. For instance, if you invest $100,000 in a 30-year bond today, the $100,000 you receive upon maturity will likely only purchase a little more than $41,000 worth of goods and services in the future.

Of course, you'd receive several times that amount in interest over the 30-year term of the loan. However, this isn't always the case when you invest in short-term fixed income investments, like CDs. Let's suppose you put $100,000 into a 12-month CD, which yields 2%. If the inflation rate is 3%, then you'll actually lose money. Sure, you'll earn $2,000 in interest but when your principal is returned to you, it will buy almost $3,000 less than it would have bought for you a year earlier. For this reason, many people define CDs as "Certificates of Depreciation".

That being said, investing in a CD is surely better than burying the money in your backyard. After all, inflation occurs regardless of where you invest your money. Therefore, it's preferable to have a return that partially offsets inflation than to have no return at all. Nevertheless, as you can see, inflation risk pushes investors to seek higher returns with longer maturity bonds, which in turn, exposes them to more interest rate risk. It's the ultimate Catch 22. This is why laddering can be such a powerful tool for fixed income investors.

Habit #4: Asset Allocation and Diversification

In the past, the common wisdom was that retirees should move all (or at least, most) of their assets out of stocks and into "safe" investments. The common rule of thumb was that the percentage of fixed income investments should be equal to the retiree's age. Under this rule, a 65-year-old man should have 65% of his assets in bonds and the remaining 35% in stocks. Likewise, an 80-year-old woman should have 80% of her assets in fixed income investments and just 20% of her assets in stock. Under this rule, each year, the percentage of assets in stock would decrease. And while it's certainly true that, in general, retirees should allocate a greater percentage of their assets to less risky investments, such as bonds or T-bills, a "one size fits all" formula is simply unworkable for today's retirees.

After all, no two retirees have the same financial situation. Some retirees have accumulated millions of dollars while others have accumulated hundreds (or maybe just tens) of thousands of dollars. Furthermore, some retirees have pensions, real estate rentals or other monthly income from which to finance their retirement lifestyles. On the other hand, some retirees must depend primarily on the income (and principal) of retirement assets. Finally, while some retirees experience a decline in monthly expenditures, others experience significant increases as they travel, start a business, enroll in school, etc.

Besides, the rapidly increasing life span of retirees is fundamentally changing the investment picture for millions of Americans. As we have discussed, retirees are living longer than ever before. As a result, their existing assets must grow at a higher rate of return in order to last during this extended time frame. For instance, let's suppose you retire at age 55 with assets of $300,000. Let's further suppose your retirement lifestyle requires you to withdraw $15,000 each year. Under this scenario (and assuming that the historically low inflation

Figure 4.6

Year	Annual Expenditures	Nest Egg Balance 2.8%	5.7%	6.9%
1	$15,000.00	$293,400.00	$302,100.00	$305,700.00
2	$15,450.00	$286,165.20	$303,869.70	$311,343.30
3	$15,913.50	$278,264.33	$305,276.77	$316,912.49
4	$16,390.91	$269,664.82	$306,286.64	$322,388.54
5	$16,882.63	$260,332.80	$306,862.35	$327,750.72
6	$17,389.11	$250,233.01	$306,964.39	$332,976.41
7	$17,910.78	$239,328.75	$306,550.58	$338,041.00
8	$18,448.11	$227,581.85	$305,575.85	$342,917.72
9	$19,001.55	$214,952.59	$303,992.13	$347,577.49
10	$19,571.60	$201,399.66	$301,748.08	$351,988.74
11	$20,158.75	$186,880.11	$298,788.98	$356,117.22
12	$20,763.51	$171,349.24	$295,056.44	$359,925.80
13	$21,386.41	$154,760.61	$290,488.24	$363,374.26
14	$22,028.01	$137,065.90	$285,018.07	$366,419.08
15	$22,688.85	$118,214.90	$278,575.25	$369,013.15
16	$23,369.51	$ 98,155.41	$271,084.53	$371,105.55
17	$24,070.60	$ 76,833.16	$262,465.75	$372,641.24
18	$24,792.71	$ 54,191.78	$252,633.58	$373,560.77
19	$25,536.50	$ 30,172.65	$241,497.20	$373,799.96
20	$26,302.59	$ 4,714.89	$228,959.95	$373,289.57
21	$27,091.67		$214,919.00	$371,954.88
22	$27,904.42		$199,264.96	$369,715.35
23	$28,741.55		$181,881.52	$366,484.16
24	$29,603.80		$162,644.97	$362,167.77
25	$30,491.91		$141,423.82	$356,665.43

Figure 4.5 *continued*

26	$31,406.67	$118,078.31	$349,868.68
27	$32,348.87	$ 92,459.90	$341,660.75
28	$33,319.34	$ 64,410.78	$331,916.00
29	$34,318.92	$ 33,763.28	$320,499.29
30	$35,348.48	$ 339.30	$307,265.26
31	$36,408.94		$292,057.63
32	$37,501.21		$274,708.40
33	$38,626.24		$255,037.04
34	$39,785.03		$232,849.56
35	$40,978.58		$207,937.60
36	$42,207.94		$180,077.36
37	$43,474.17		$149,028.53
38	$44,778.40		$114,533.09
39	$46,121.75		$ 76,314.12
40	$47,505.40		$ 34,074.39

rate holds), your money must grow at just 2.8% per year to last 20 years until the age of 75. However, if you want to stretch those same assets for 30 years (or until the age of 85), you must earn an annual return of 5.7%. And if you want to stretch those same assets for 40 years (age 95), you must earn 6.0% per year on your money.

Many retirees are seeking the higher investment returns that stocks can provide … and for good reason. Since 1925, stocks have provided higher returns than most other investment vehicles. In fact, $10,000 invested in the S&P 500

Index each year since 1934 would've been worth nearly $15,000,000 in December of 2002.[ii] For this reason, some advisors are now recommending that retirees allocate a percentage of their assets to fixed income investments that represents their age *minus* 20. Therefore, under this new rule, a 75-year-old retiree would allocate 55% of his assets to fixed income investments and the remaining 45% in stocks.

Of course, asset allocation is just a piece of diversification. In addition to owning different classes of assets (e.g., stocks, bonds, notes, etc.), a retirement investor should also be well diversified within each of these classes. As we've discussed earlier, laddering bond maturities is a good way to mitigate the interest rate risk associated with owning bonds.

On the stock side of the equation, diversification is even more important. Obviously, almost no one would consider owning just one stock in their portfolio due to the adage "don't put all of your eggs in one basket." Therefore, an investor should own a variety of different stocks. This partly explains the popularity of mutual funds. They allow investors of all sizes to own literally hundreds of stocks when such a diverse ownership of stocks would be impossible to all but the wealthiest investors.

However, it's important not to confuse owning a mutual fund with true diversification. For instance, placing all of your stock assets in a telecommunications mutual fund is not my idea of diversification. Surely, it's better than just having all of your money in AT&T. Yet, industry specific mutual funds expose the investor to the very real risk that this particularly sector of the market will suffer a downturn or lose favor with investors.

In addition to diversifying among industries, you should diversity among the various styles of stock mutual funds. One such style is the growth funds which invest in those companies with the perceived greatest promise of experiencing significant growth in the near future. On the other hand, there are value mutual funds, which invest in larger companies with proven track records. The prospect for the significant growth among these companies is less than the growth for their counterparts. And finally, there are funds that take a blended approach. These funds invest in both value and growth stocks.

Also, in some cases, geographic diversification is warranted. Despite the political risk, foreign stocks can be a good investment because seldom is the U.S. stock market the single best performing market in any given year. In fact, over the period from 1993 until 2002, the U.S. wasn't the #1 performing market in the world once.[iii]

In some years, the performance of the U.S. stock market was just plain awful in comparison to some of its foreign counterparts. For example, in 2001 and 2002, the S&P 500 index lost 12% and 22%, respectively. However, over those same two years, the New Zealand stock market *gained* 8% and 24%, respectively. And even during some good recent years, the U.S. stock market has been outperformed by some foreign markets. For instance, in 1995, the S&P 500 rose a whopping 38%. Yet, that same year, the Swiss markets rose 44%. Likewise, in 1999, the S&P index rose a very respectable 21%. Yet, this return was dwarfed by the 153% increase in Finland's stock market.

Of course, all of this does NOT mean that you should take your money out of the U.S. stock market. Over the long term, the U.S. stock market has produced very favorable returns. However, investing in foreign markets does represent an opportunity to share in the returns of the hottest stock markets in any given year. This strategy can prove particularly advantageous during periods when the U.S. stock market is undergoing a bear market.

It's important to note that a truly diversified portfolio of investments won't provide the greatest return during any given year. For instance, if growth stocks are performing well in a particular year, then a diversified portfolio holder won't do as well as someone who is heavily concentrated in growth stocks. Nevertheless, over time, a diversified portfolio should provide for a solid overall return because it won't be subject to fluctuations as extreme as would be encountered in a non-diversified portfolio. And as demonstrated above, a more stable and consistent rate of growth produces better long-term results than investments with wildly fluctuating returns.

Five Common Mistakes of Retirement Investing

In addition to following the four habits of wealthy retirement investors, it's important to avoid the five most common mistakes of retirement investing.

1. Leaving too much Money in Company Stock
2. Leaving Too Much in Cash
3. Poor Diversification Strategies
4. No Vision (Piece Meal Assembly of a Portfolio)
5. Changing Strategies Too Often

Leaving Too Much Money in Company Stock

For retirees who accumulated a sizable portion of their assets through company stock and stock options, it can be difficult to let go of a familiar "friend." After all, in many cases, the retiree may have been holding this stock for 10, 20, or 30 years. Making the decision to part with the stock can be heart-wrenching; particularly, when the person has fond attachments to the company and his or her many years of service there.

However, holding a large percentage of your assets in any one vehicle is incredibly risky. This is particularly the case for a retiree who may no longer have access to current information about the company that could shed some light on its near-term and long-term viability. Furthermore, even those within the company can be taken by surprise. A perfect example of this occurred with the employees of Enron, WorldCom, and other companies, who, in recent years, have seen a large portion of their retirement assets disappear into thin air.

Leaving Too Much in Cash

In most cases, the inflation-adjusted return of CDs, money markets and passbook savings accounts are negative. Every retiree needs to include a portion of stocks and bonds for the opportunity to "grow" their money. Yet, while many retirees realize this fact, moving their money out of bank accounts and CDs is difficult.

One factor that contributes to this problem is fear. While market risk, credit risks, interest rate risks, and political risks can be reduced, they can't be entirely eliminated. Faced with the possibility of losing some or all of their assets in capital markets, some retirees decide that they'd rather not take **any** chances. Of course, in doing so, they often run the ultimate risk – the risk that they will eventually run out of money because inflation has eaten away at the purchasing power of their existing assets.

The second factor is procrastination. Please understand that this isn't willful or even careless procrastination. Instead, in many cases, the retiree is genuinely interested in entering the market but is waiting for the "perfect" time. As we all know, there simply is no perfect time to invest (or do anything else for that matter). Hindsight will always demonstrate that there was a better time to do this or do that. Fortunately, as discussed earlier in this chapter, you need not be perfect in order to earn solid returns in the market so long as you recognize that time (and not timing) is on your side. Regardless of your age the best time is now.

Poor Diversification Strategies

Often, in an attempt to diversity, investors simply spread their assets among the same class of funds. For instance, an investor may divide the stock portion of his assets between 10 different mutual funds. However, if each fund is similar in its focus (e.g., they are all large growth funds), then the purpose of diversification has been somewhat defeated. The key to effective diversification is to not only spread assets among different investments but also among investment classes.

No Vision (Piece Meal Assembly of a Portfolio)

Ideally, each individual investment should be a piece to an overall investment picture. Taken as a whole, your investments should give you the greatest opportunity to reach your goals during retirement. However, often times, this isn't the way that investments are accumulated.

For instance, we talked earlier about how some people acquire a large part of their assets in the form of company stock. This isn't part of some master financial plan. In addition, sometimes investments are made on the basis of a "hot tip." The retiree hears about a particular stock in the barber shop, in the beauty salon, TV, or radio and decides to buy a few hundred (or thousand) shares on a whim.

Of course, the problem here is that these "random" investments detract from an otherwise balanced portfolio. Ideally, each investment should be made only after careful consideration and be part of an overall diversified package.

Changing Strategies Too Often

While all investors should monitor their investments on a regular basis, they should be careful not to change strategies or advisors too often. There will be up times and down times in any portfolio. The key is not to panic during the down times. Over time, most balanced portfolios should provide a respectable return but sometimes it takes just that; time. It's very hard to think rational during irrational times. However with an overall strategy you have addressed the down times before they ever occurred.

For instance, over the better part of the last century, there was a 28% chance that the general market would be down in any one year. However, there was only a 10% chance that the general market would be down over any five-year period. Over a 10-year period, the chances of losing money dropped to 3%. And never in history, has the U.S. stock market been down for any 15-year period. While past performance is no guarantee of future results, this shows once again, it's important to invest for the long-term.[iv]

[i] Geoffrey A. Moore, *The Gorilla Game, Revised Edition*

[ii] Source: Lipper as of 12/31/03.

[iii] Source: RIMES Technologies Corp. and Bloomberg.

[iv] 2000 Stocks, Bonds, Bills, and Inflation Yearbook.

— CHAPTER 5 —

YOUR BROKER CAN MAKE YOU… BROKER

As a retiree, you must take special care to avoid poor investments. As we discussed earlier, you don't have a luxury of working another 10, 20, or 30 years to rebuild your nest egg. One serious mistake and you could spend your Golden years working at the Golden Arches! Unless you love flipping burgers, you should carefully evaluate the risks and features of an investment before you invest. Make no mistake; all investments your broker may show you may **NOT** be great choices for you. You must take the time to understand how these investments relate to you and your plan.

Some investments are aggressively marketed by brokers and financial planners in part because they pay large commissions. In some cases, the commission can be up to 10% of your principal. And in many cases, the commission is 5-7% of the amount invested. As you may guess, they can be particularly attractive to brokers and financial planners. After all, if you invested $500,000 in one of these investments with a 7% commission, the broker would earn $35,000 in commissions. That's not a bad day's work!

Of course, I'm not suggesting that there are many financial planners who would intentionally stick you with a bad investment to make a quick buck (although, sadly, there are certainly a few who would). However, the large commissions involved make it sometimes difficult for even the most honest professional to evaluate the investment. I'm devoting this chapter of the book to objectively explaining the pros and especially the cons of most of these investments.

Please also note that I'm not suggesting that these types of investments are inappropriate. Each of these investments can be particularly effective in the right circumstances, even for retirees. Unfortunately, these investments may be recommended to investors that may not see great benefits from their use. Production goals, manager's expectations and winning company trips can often trump good product selection. Please, please travel carefully down this road. Sometimes, the road less traveled is less traveled for a reason.

Annuity Products

Annuity products are investment vehicles offered by insurance companies. There are two types of annuities- fixed and variable. As the name implies, fixed annuities pay interest at a fixed rate, which is typically higher than the rates paid by banks. The insurance company takes your money and invests it. The principal and return of a fixed annuity are guaranteed by the issuing company and both are solely based on the claims paying ability of that particular company. With variable annuities, the investor invests their money in variable sub-accounts that are often "clones" of mutual funds. The sub-accounts may be similar to stock funds, the S&P 500, bond funds or many other variable investments. As an investor, one needs to research the sub-accounts and find appropriate investments to help reach your goals. The principal and return of the variable annuity sub accounts are not guaranteed and is subject to market risks including possible loss of your principal.

A major selling point for annuities is their tax deferral. Therefore, instead of paying taxes each year on your interest or capital gains, gains are taxed as ordinary income upon withdrawal from your annuity. Annuities are afforded this special tax treatment because they are both insurance product and an investment product. Most annuities offer several annuitization options. These options are similar to a company's pension plan. The annuity will offer a series of monthly payments that will be for your lifetime or selected time frame. Certain companies guarantee a certain return on your money or at least the return of your principal within a certain time period regardless of market performance. All guarantees are based on the claims paying ability of the issuing company.

In the case of variable annuities, any guarantee of principal and/or return are offered through riders and will carry additional charges. Be careful, these charges can add up. Make sure you understand the total amount of charges. Fees can top 3% per year and a 3% annual fee can impact your return significantly.

While there are many benefits to investing in annuities, these benefits are often overstated. For one, although you may receive a "guaranteed" rate of return, the question again is guaranteed by whom? Again, this point bears repeating. Your money is guaranteed by the claims paying ability of the company who issued the contract. Therefore, if you invest a significant portion of your assets in a weak insurance company, it is possible to lose most or even your entire principal if the company is unable to meet its obligations. This is true even if the underlying investments have performed well. Therefore, even an investment in a US treasury could be at risk if it is inside an annuity.

Fortunately, insurance companies operate under a stringent legal reserve system. At all times, insurance companies must maintain assets in excess of their liabilities. This is in contrast to banks, which must only maintain assets representing a few pennies for every dollar of their obligations. As a result, many insurance companies are generally more stable. Of course, one great protection afforded to bank depositors is FDIC insurance on deposit accounts such as checking, savings account and certificate of deposits. The FDIC guarantees the first $100,000 per depositor per insured bank. There is no similar protection available to annuity holders.

Most professionals recommend that you select top-rated companies in which to invest. In fact, when insurance products, they will often point to the strength of the insurer, touting the insurer's assets under management, financial ratings, and years in the business. The problem with all these measures is that they are only current measures. They say nothing about how well the insurer will be doing in 10 or 20 years when you come back to collect your money. And as we've all witnessed over the last 20 years, even the largest and most stable insurers can experience difficulties. A present example of this is the trouble experienced in the 1990's by one of the world's largest and most revered insurer, Lloyd's of London. Operating history is important but understand you must take the lead in keeping track of current ratings and standings of the company's strength EVERY year.

While I briefly mentioned this earlier, it bears repeating again. Tax deferred earnings should never be confused with tax-free earnings. Taxes will be paid either when you withdraw funds or upon your death. Nevertheless, this can certainly be preferable to paying taxes on funds that are sitting in an account somewhere. I tell clients frequently, there is no sense on paying taxes on money you're not using. Tax Deferral has its benefits….but it's not the cure-all some advisors make it out to be.

For some investors, the tax-deferred aspect of annuities is nullified by their need to withdraw funds each year. In this case, the annuity returns are effectively taxed just as if the money had been earning interest on a bond or in a bank. In addition to taxes, early withdrawals may be subject to surrender charges and if made before 59 ½ may also be subject to a 10% IRA penalty. Furthermore, the annuity holder is still subject to not only the normal management fees but also added insurance expenses. In short, tax-deferral is only a meaningful benefit for those retirees who don't have an active need for the income being produced in the annuity. Sadly, this fact isn't always made clear to the retired investor.

The final argument for annuities: They provide a measure of protection to the retiree. For instance, many fixed annuities provide for a minimum guaranteed rate of return (again, the guarantee is based on the claims paying ability of the insurance company). Likewise, many variable annuities will guarantee a certain rate of return, or at least guarantee that the retiree will receive her principal back. Obviously, these guarantees aren't available if you invest your funds in the market unless you pay additional fees through certain riders. Make sure you take time to understand any rider you may purchase. Often times, to utilize the rider you must jump through hoops that aren't made clear by the advisor. If it sounds too good to be true, then guess what, it usually is....learn about the rider BEFORE you purchase it. Preservation of capital is perhaps the primary concern of most retirees. This feature of annuities can be extremely attractive. However one must take ample time to study the many options available. This is because there are so many different variables to consider.

Most annuity investors must decide whether to annuitize or not. In other words, they must choose whether to receive a guaranteed series of payments over a certain period of time or whether to receive a lump-sum amount when they choose to withdraw funds. Furthermore, this decision can be complicated because the retiree will have several options – they can receive their funds over 5, 10, or 20 years or even their lifetimes. Comparing all of the options and their various internal rates of returns can be confusing enough in a fixed annuity. However, it becomes even more difficult when dealing with variable annuities, which provide a far-reaching range of protections. For instance, some variable annuities may guarantee the return of your original deposit within a certain period of time (through certain riders). Therefore, even if the market crashes, the insurance company will return the entire amount of your principal if you qualify through your optional rider. In addition, some variable annuities guarantee a positive rate of return if you annuitize your payout. For such riders, the insurance company might pay you the greater of your guaranteed return or the amount you are entitled from the annuitization of your investment account.

Finally, all annuities have with it a death benefit. Usually, upon your death, your heirs are entitled to receive the accumulated value of your account. Most annuities will guarantee your death benefit to be at least as much as your original investment. Other annuities will even guarantee that your benefit increases a certain percentage (say 5%) each year, regardless of the performance of your portfolio inside the annuity.

These guaranteed living and death benefits are obviously helpful to the retiree and few argue otherwise. However, some critics argue that the price for these benefits is often just too high. In order to guarantee your returns, the insurance company must charge a fee to offset for the risk that your investments will fall. This fee can be as high as 2.5% annually. Of course, the "proper" amounts of these fees are purely a matter of conjecture. They depend upon several variables – the outlook for the market's performance during the applicable period, mortality figures, etc. Therefore, even actuaries can't agree on the "proper" fee to adequately compensate the insurer for taking on this market risk. Few retirees (or even their advisors) are in a good position to determine whether they're overpaying for this coverage.

I would be remiss not to discuss a very controversial aspect of many annuities: The surrender charge. In some annuities, the investor is charged a fee for withdrawing funds within a certain period of time (e.g., within the first 3-10 years). Obviously, the purpose of this surrender charge is to create an incentive for you to stay invested in the annuity. Your continued enrollment in the annuity provides a reliable source of management and insurance fees to the insurer. In fairness, it also allows the fund managers to manage with a much longer-term focus.

To encourage you to stay longer, the insurance companies provide a financial incentive to brokers and financial planners to market annuities with longer surrender charges. A financial professional can earn up to 7% in commissions for selling an annuity with a surrender charge that extends to the 7th year or longer. If you don't have a foreseeable use for the money, your broker may argue that this type of annuity offers increased benefits, so why not?

However, there is a strong argument against long surrender charges – unforeseen expenses. Sure, your current financial position may indicate that you don't need to touch the money for seven years but what if things change? For example, what if you or your spouse requires medical treatment or hospitalization that isn't covered by your existing health insurance? Do you really want to pay a fee to have access to your money? Particularly, when you consider that this fee, combined with the taxes you'll owe upon withdrawing your funds, you may eat up a substantial amount of your return.

For instance, let's suppose that you are 59 ½ or older and you've invested $100,000 in a fixed annuity with a 4% return and that you have to make an early withdrawal of the entire amount after four years at a surrender charge of 4%. In this case, your initial investment has grown to $116,985.86. However, after paying your surrender charge, you are left with just $112,306.42. Furthermore, assuming you are taxed at a 32% marginal rate, after taxes, you will retain just $108,368.37. As a result, your effective rate of return would be just over 2%. In other words, surrender charges and taxes would eat up almost half of the total return (in this example.)

Illiquid Investments

Since no one has a crystal ball into the future, it's important to build some flexibility into your investments. Surely, you don't want to jump from investment to investment (more on that later) but on the other hand, you should have the flexibility to be able to make adjustments to your portfolio when long-term market shifts occur or when your personal situation changes. You should be wary of investments that tie up your funds indefinitely or for years at a time.

One example of an illiquid investment is a **limited partnership interest**. In many industries, limited partnerships are formed for such purposes as aircraft leasing, oil and gas exploration, real estate, and the list goes on and on. Sadly, retirees have been the target of numerous limited partnership scams. Nevertheless, there are many legitimate (not to mention potentially lucrative) opportunities to invest in limited partnerships. Yet, regardless of the nature of the investment, the illiquidity of limited partnerships should give any retiree **concern** about making such investment.

In a limited partnership, the power of the limited partners is just that; limited. All decisions about the operation of the company are made by the general partner. In addition, the general partner usually has the sole discretion to determine when, and if, income is to be distributed to the partners. No limited partner has the right to insist that the partnership pay a dividend or repurchase his shares. As a result, the limited partners are largely at the mercy of the general partner to receive funds from the partnership.

Of course, in one sense, a limited partnership interest isn't much different from a shareholder interest in a public corporation. Unless you are a significant shareholder, you can't force the CEO to resign or force the company to enter into the baby food market. Likewise, you can't force the Board of Directors to declare a dividend or to initiate a stock buyback program. However, as the shareholder in a public company, you do have one important option – you can always terminate your investment by selling your shares in the open market and receiving the current market price which may equal less or possibly more than all your original investment.

Unfortunately, this isn't the case with limited partnership interests. Limited partnerships are seldom publicly traded on a national exchange or over the counter market. In these cases, the only way to get your money back would be to find a buyer for your interests. And, of course, this assumes that your limited partnership will allow you to sell your interests, which isn't always the case. Furthermore, you will have to comply with a myriad of rules to make sure that your sale doesn't violate state and federal securities laws. In short, selling interests in a private limited partnership can be extremely difficult. If your broker casually mentions limited partnership when reviewing investment options, take a very close look and make sure you understand what you may enter into!

Another potentially illiquid investment is the unit investment trust (UIT). Unit investment trusts are similar to traditional mutual funds in that they allow for the investor to diversify his holdings by pooling his money with other investors to purchase securities. However, unlike the open-ended mutual fund that allows the investor to purchase or sell shares at any time, unit investment trusts are **closed-end funds**. Once the fund has been formed, the number of "units" is fixed. UIT's are created for a set term, they do not exist indefinitely. If new investors want to enter the trust, they must purchase existing units from an existing holder. Likewise, if current holders want to exit the trust early, they must sell their units to a new investor.

While this may seem unduly restrictive, there is actually a logical reason for keeping the number of units static. It allows the trust to buy and hold securities for a set period of time. In an open-ended fund, the managers must continually buy and sell shares to employ newly received funds and to pay for redemptions. However, in a unit investment trust, the managers can buy a portfolio of securities on the date the fund is formed and hold the securities indefinitely (based on the guidelines on the UIT).

This allows unit investment trusts to employ some strategies that are simply not available to open-ended mutual funds. A good example of such a strategy is the much heralded Dogs of the Dow strategy. The theory behind the Dogs of the Dow strategy is to buy one share of each of the 10 stocks on the Dow Jones Industrial Average paying the highest dividend (as a percentage of stock prices). In fact, according to **dogsofthedow.com**, the strategy has returned 17.7% average annual return since 1973. Over the same time period, the Dow achieved an average annual return of 11.9%. However, past performance is no guarantee of future success. In any given year, the Dogs of the Dow strategy may lose money or underperform the market.

There are other advantages of unit investment trusts. For one, the investor is not taxed on the gain of the trust but rather on realized gains through dividends and capital gains. Second, the management costs are usually minimal in a unit investment trust because the portfolio remains fairly static. Correspondingly, trading costs are also kept to a minimum.

Yet, these advantages of investing in unit investment trusts may not be enough to overcome the disadvantage of poor liquidity. While many of these closed-end funds trade on the exchanges, they usually trade at a slight discount to their asset value. This is because many investors prefer to invest their funds in open-ended mutual funds, where they can easily cash out their investment at any time. Furthermore, investing in unit investment trusts often requires paying a brokerage commission to both buy and sell the units.

When considering the pros and cons, it may make sense for some investors to only consider unit investment trusts that have very short life spans and that should have adequate trading volume. For instance, Dogs of the Dow trusts usually last only for a year. The portfolio is purchased on the first trading day of the year and sold on the last trading day of the year and the funds are distributed to investors. If you can stand to have your money tied up for just a short period of time (probably no longer than 2-4 years), this can be a viable investment option. Otherwise, it may make sense to invest in open-ended mutual funds.

Another likely illiquid investment is the real estate investment trust or REIT. As the name implies, REITs invest in a portfolio of income producing properties, usually shopping malls and office buildings. The benefits of REITs are that they allow you to invest in real estate assets without the headaches of actually managing the properties. Furthermore, REITs are pass through vehicles; they pass through cash flows without paying a corporate tax on those assets. As a result, the investor doesn't experience the double taxation that accompanies receiving distributions from a corporation.

Furthermore, the dividends paid by REITs can be considerably higher. According to the National Association of REITs (NAREIT), over the last 10 years (1995-2005), the average dividend of the NAREIT composite was 6.98% versus the dividend of the S&P 500 of 1.57%!

Another advantage of investing in REITs is that they are more liquid than owning the real estate outright. To liquidate your investment, you don't have to list a property with a realtor and wait the 3-6 months that might normally attend the closing of a real estate transaction. Instead, you simply sell your interest in the trust to a third party. As many REITs are publicly traded, this is often as simple as placing a sell order with your stockbroker.

Yet, while REITs may be more liquid than the underlying real estate assets it holds, they are significant less liquid than other investments, such as common stock in publicly traded corporations like AT&T and Microsoft. Most REIT shares are thinly traded in the market. As a result, if you hold a significant number of shares in a REIT, it may be difficult to sell them all at once (at least without significant depressing the market price of those shares).

Variable Universal Life

Under a universal variable life policy, your annual premiums are placed into a general account. After deducting the cost of insurance and other costs of the insurer, the remainder of the premium is invested in sub accounts of your choosing. The funds in your general account grow tax-deferred and can even be used to pay for future annual premiums. Because these policies combine insurance with investments, some financial professionals push them as a way to "kill two birds with one stone."

Unfortunately, if you're not extremely careful, you and your spouse may be the "birds" in question because the up-front sales cost and annual expenses can be "killers." Furthermore, your investments will be likely limited to a very small universe of the insurer's proprietary funds. Therefore, you can be effectively locked out of some investment opportunities with greater potential.

Many financial advisors suggest that you separate insurance from investments. Of course, this advice is most applicable to younger people, who can buy term life insurance at a fraction of the cost of universal life insurance. For many retirees, the cost of term insurance can be prohibitive. Of course, at an advance age, so is the cost of universal life insurance. Do you need to protect your spouse or create a legacy? You need to decide if you need an **investment** OR purchase **life insurance**. Remember, determine where you are trying to go and then choose the right vehicle to take you there!

Nevertheless, many people seem to get confused about the purpose of life insurance, which is to replace your income for your family if you should die or possibly pay for large sum of taxes for their estate. Therefore, as a general rule, your need for life insurance should be less as you enter retirement because most of your income should come from investments and not your physical labor. For this reason, acquiring new life insurance as a retiree should probably be lower on your list of concerns.

The only exception is if you need to use life insurance to pay estate taxes, which will be discussed at length in a later chapter. However, even in that situation, give some careful consideration to the cost and fees associated with any universal variable life insurance policy. Remember, the fortune you save could be your own.

SALES CHARGES AND COMMISSIONS

Sometimes your broker's priorities don't line up with your priorities (in terms of your investments). This can be the case when your broker is locked into only offering the mutual funds managed by her firm. Sure, her firm may offer many fine mutual funds but the best fund for you in terms of potential performance, risk, and objectives may be a fund offered by a competing firm. In this case, your broker simply can't offer you the best product on the market.

One way to address the potential for the proprietary fund conflict is to choose a financial professional who has access to a wide range of investments. In my opinion **independent brokerage firms** provide such access. That way, you have a better chance that the broker will look at funds outside of her firm's funds. One way to make sure that your broker is really taking a look at the big picture is to ask questions about competing funds. For instance, if your broker sits down and tells you all about a great investment, you could ask, "Can you give me the name of some other good funds in this category?" If she can't do this, then you know that she hasn't been shopping for you. If she does give you some other funds, then ask for some information about these funds so that you can do some comparison shopping.

This is particularly important when dealing with mutual funds with high front-end and back-end loads, or sales charges. Some funds that are distributed directly to the public typically add no sales charges up front. These funds are called "no load" funds. However, many funds charge either a front-end or back-end load. In other words, you pay a sales charge to enter the fund or at the time you leave the fund. For those funds with back-end loads, the charge usually decreases every year until at some point, there is no back-end load. For instance, some funds will charge a 5% sales charge if you leave within the first year, but that charge will decrease by 1%

each year until after the fifth or sixth year, when there is no sales charge for leaving the fund.

While the amount of the sales charge may seem small, it can make a big difference in the long-run. With a front-end load fund, only a portion of your investment actually goes to work for you. The sales charge is deducted from the amount you invest and paid directly to the broker. Over the long-term, this can make a small difference in your return on investment, For example, let's suppose you invest $10,000 in a no-load fund and another $10,000 in a front-end load fund with a 4% sales charge. Therefore, in the first fund, all of your $10,000 will be invested but in the second fund, just $9,600 will be invested after deducting the $400 sales charge. Let's further suppose that both funds earn annual returns of 10% per year.

After 10 years, your no-load fund investment would be worth $25,937.43 while your load fund investment would be worth just $24,899.93, a difference of more than $1,000. After 20 years, the difference is even more pronounced. Your no-load fund investment would be worth $67,274.99 while your load fund investment would be worth just $64,584.00, a difference of almost $2,700. And after 30 years, this difference is even greater. Your no-load fund investment would be worth $174,494.02 while your load fund investment would be worth just $167,514.26. As you can see, a mere $400 sales charge results in a difference in total returns of almost $7,000 over 30 years. Of course, this is a hypothetical example and not representative of any specific investment. Your results could vary.

While it may seem like a simple solution to only invest in "no load" funds, it isn't quite that easy. Over the past decade, an increasing number of mutual funds have begun imposing 12b-1 distribution and service fees. Through the imposition of these fees, funds are able to reduce their front and back-end loads and still compensate brokers by using this fee to pay sales commissions. Furthermore, as these fees are imposed every year you own the fund, over time, they may exceed the amount you would have spent by just paying the load up-front. Be careful it's necessary to read the fund's prospectus carefully before investing to determine just how much of a sales charge you will be paying. **I'm not saying you shouldn't pay fees. However, I believe investors should be aware of the fees.** Advisors should be compensated...but compensated fairly and the advisor should take the time to explain how they are going to earn their compensation.

One way to reduce the effects of loads is to invest more money. Most funds have breakpoints above which the load decreases. For instance, a fund may have the following front-end load schedule:

Figure 5.1

Amount Invested	Load
Up to $10,000	4%
$10,001-$20,000	3%
$20,001-$50,000	2%
$50,001-$100,000	1%
Over $100,000	No load

Using the above example, an investment of $19,000 into the fund would entail a sales charge of $570, while an investment of $20,001 would entail a sales charge of just $400.02. Therefore, by investing an extra $1,001 into the fund, you would obtain the benefit of an additional $1,170.98 working for you (additional $1001 principal invested and $169.98 saved in load charges). Therefore, it makes sense to watch for these breakpoints and to structure your investments so that they take advantage of these breakpoints.

If your broker is compensated solely by commissions, these breakpoints can serve as an incentive to do the opposite. For example, let's suppose that you have $30,000 to invest in international stocks. Using the above breakpoints, if you invested the entire amount in one fund, you would pay a 3% sales charge or $900. However, if you were to split your investment between two funds, your total sales charge of 4% would total $1,200. Of course, most conscientious brokers will inform you about breakpoints and attempt to structure your investment to take advantage of them. Nevertheless, you can protect yourself by making sure that you obtain this information before making any investment decisions.

Another way to reduce your sales charge: Make trades within the same mutual fund family, most fund companies don't charge a load for switches within their family of funds. Therefore, if you decide that you need to further diversify your holdings, inquire as to whether the fund you are switching out of has a "sister" fund that invests in the new area. Of course, the load should never be your primary concern but all things being equal, you should attempt to conduct transactions within the same fund family to save on sales charges.

In fact, for this reason, it may make sense to restrict your mutual fund purchases to those funds that are affiliated with a broad range of other funds. While an isolated fund may have achieved stellar performance in the past, the opportunity to participate in the potential future performance may be offset by future sales charges you will incur if you need to switch into another fund family in the future.

Once again, your broker should inform you about all of these factors but, if he is a commission-based broker, his financial incentive isn't to do so. He's compensated on the basis of the sales charges you pay. Therefore, a little caution on your part is prudent. **In my opinion, how well a fund meets your objectives and risk tolerance as well as potential performance is more important than fees.** Lets put this another way. What kind of car do you drive? I'm sure you said a Hyundai....right? After all it's the least expensive. As you can see, we don't make all decisions based solely on EXPENSES....**your investments should be no different**!

Another situation in which brokers have conflicting interests: Receiving higher compensation for pushing their firm's offerings. This is particularly true when the brokerage firm is underwriting a new stock that it's having trouble moving into the market. In that case, the firm may create additional incentives for brokers to move the securities in the form of trips, gift certificates, and other perks. These perks give the broker an additional incentive to push products that may be less than stellar for you.

As a general rule, you should be wary of new stocks unless they are secondary offerings. As an investor interested in avoiding as much financial risk as possible, your general strategy probably will be to "wait and see." Of course, there will be times when a new stock is just what you've been looking for. Probably the best way to judge your broker's true intentions is to ask yourself if the offering fits into your general strategy. If you normally invest in established companies and you get a call from your broker to invest in a new biotech stock, your broker may be just trying to win a new set of golf clubs!

Past Star Performers

In helping you to choose the proper fund in which to invest, your broker may rely too heavily on ratings. While these ratings are certainly helpful, by definition, they don't tell the whole story. Why? Because the ratings are based upon past performance. Those funds that have performed best in the past are the highest rated. Of course, on the one hand, this makes perfect sense. On the other hand, the view is somewhat limited and can lead to disappointment. After all, you drive looking through your car's windshield not the rear view mirror, right?

In every piece of literature that you receive from a financial firm (including my own), you will find the following disclaimer: "Past performance is no guarantee of future results." That disclosure is there for a reason; because it's true. The fact that a fund was the top performer in its class last year is no guarantee that it will be the top performer this year or next year.

In fact, strong past performance can be a hindrance in some cases. This is what happened to Fidelity's legendary Magellan Fund. During the 1980s, the fund racked up an impressive investment record. As a result, it became the darling of investors everywhere. The fund enjoyed so much success that its manager, Peter Lynch, went on to become a national celebrity, best-selling author, and money management guru. In my opinion, this success proved to be the downfall for the fund.

As more and more investors rushed to "get in on a good thing," the fund had trouble keeping itself fully invested. As an increasing percentage of funds sat in money market accounts, the overall performance of the fund decreased. Furthermore, in order to invest all of the funds under management, the fund managers had to buy stocks that they may not have otherwise purchase. In all, the fund was unable to keep up its winning ways.

Besides, even under normal circumstances, the performance of a fund will vacillate from year to year. It happens, its normal. Perhaps, the fund manager is really good on capitalizing on a bull market but not so good at surviving a bear market, or vice versa. Or perhaps, managers leave the fund. Turnover is particularly high in this industry. The point is simply that neither you nor your advisor should choose a fund solely on the basis of past performance because things change.

In fact, there is a growing sentiment among financial professionals that many investors should avoid managed funds altogether. The simple truth of the matter is that a majority of stock funds underperform their relevant market index. While, at first glance, this may seem unbelievable or even an indictment of the mutual fund industry, it's actually the way things have to be.

After all, by definition, only about half of the fund managers should be able to beat the indexes and the other half of the managers should lose to the indexes. However, this doesn't take into account the expenses of running a mutual fund (e.g., trading expenses, salaries, sales commissions, administrative expenses, etc.). As a result, even if a fund manager is able to perform at the level of the indexes, the funds return could be less because of the extra expense.

Some suggest investing your money into index funds. Since index funds simply invest in a basket of stocks with an objective of representing a particular index, the expenses are minimal. Furthermore, the sales charges and other expenses are generally reduced. The simple thought process here is why should investors pay higher fees when most funds aren't going to beat the indexes anyway? Of course, while the goal/objective of an index fund is to match the performance of the index, there is not guarantee it will do so. However, that's still a very powerful question. I believe in actively managed funds. Used properly actively managed funds can help reduce risk. But for the vast majority of "do-it-yourselfers" index funds can do just fine. I also advise my clients, I don't buy actively managed funds to outperform the index, I buy actively managed funds to protect their portfolio in the event of a "bad" or bear market. There is absolutely no guarantee active management of your funds will protect you during this downturn, but certain managers have done quite well. Remember, past performance does not guarantee future success. I make these statements because you should be educated on both sides of the coin". Work with your advisor to see what's best for you.

When investing in individual stocks, the adage that "past performance is no guarantee of future results" is even more apt. Often times, an investor will be convinced to buy a stock because the broker points out the stock's performance over the last year, two years or five years. However, such advice ignores an important fact: A stocks future performance is based on the future financial performance of the company. In regards to individual stocks, some of the best advice ever given is the following: Stock prices follow earnings! As a retiree THINK TWICE ABOUT investing in companies that don't have earnings. Future earnings are great… but it's tough to pay the bills on future earnings and promises!

Besides, the stellar past performance of a stock could mean that it's overvalued and ready for a correction. As discussed earlier, stock prices fluctuate. They are up and then they are down. This is the case even when the underlying company is stable and produces predictable results. Therefore, there is always a chance that a high flying stock is just at the top of the wave and may come crashing back down to earth.

The important question is not "What has the stock done in the past?" The important question is "What are the future prospects for the company?" If your broker can't articulate a case for the future of the company, it's likely that he's just following the crowd. Don't let him lead you to the possible "slaughter".

The "Stock Tip"

Another thing to be concerned about is the stock tip. If you get a call from your broker saying, "I just heard a great tip about XYZ Company … it's going to double," then find a polite (or not so polite) way to end the call. **As a retiree, you should never buy on rumors or tips**. Actually, no investor should buy stock on this basis, but as someone who doesn't have the luxury of another 40 years of work to pay for your mistakes, you should avoid them at all cost. As Mark Twain once said, "There are two times in a man's life when he should not speculate on stocks: when he can't afford it, and when he can."

Buying on rumors and tips is nothing more than speculating. Nine times out of ten the rumor is completely unfounded. In fact, the person who tells you about the rumor is only repeating something he heard repeated by someone who heard it from someone else. These rumors are almost always false. In fact, for your sake, you should hope they are false. Otherwise, you stand more to lose than mere money. With the proliferation of the internet, stock tips are as close as a click of your mouse. It's tempting…very tempting. My experience …do it and you lose it. You developed your financial life plan for a reason. Follow it.

As you may or may not know, it's a serious offense to trade on the basis of inside information. Therefore, if your broker calls you with reliable inside information and you use that information to either make money or avoid losing money, you could find yourself being questioned by the SEC and the FBI. Needless to say, for a few thousand dollars of profit, it simply isn't worth it. Ask Martha Stewart…..enough said!

Likewise, you should avoid penny stocks. Penny stocks offer a false illusion of hope because it's so easy to imagine incredible returns. For instance, it's easy to imagine a $0.10 stock trading at $1.00 in a few short months. After all, it's just an increase of $0.90. How hard could that be? However, since this represents a 1,000% return on investment, it's easy to get caught up in this type of thinking. Particularly, if you receive an excited call from your broker telling you that you are going to make a "killing."

However, you must remember that there's a good reason why these stocks are trading at such low prices; they simply aren't worth much. As a result, since the major exchanges don't list penny stocks, you run the risk of buying into an illiquid investment. While millions of shares of a large public company like GE trade will trade each day, shares of an over-the-counter stock may not trade at all in a particular day. Or, if they do trade, the number of shares exchanging hands may be in the hundreds or low thousands. It's bad enough to get talked into buying a penny stock but it's much worse to get stuck with it.

Broker recommendations concerning hot stocks, penny stocks, and other investments aren't always made with the client's best interest at heart. In some cases, the broker is simply looking for a way to generate fees. For a commission-only broker, the only way to generate income is to engage in transactions. As these types of transactions are short-term in nature, they present a great opportunity to earn additional fees on a consistent basis.

Aside from greed, these recommendations may be made out of a sense of adventure. Rather than measuring performance in terms of years, performance in these investments is often measured in terms of days (if not hours). This can be wonderfully exciting for the broker, particularly when his life savings **aren't** at risk. However, if your broker is looking for excitement, then invite him to the horse track or the local casino, which is the proper place to take such gambles. 30 years of work can be lost in a matter of days, **UNDERSTAND YOUR INVESTMENTS**!

Your Broker Can Make You ... Broker

To recap, while the vast majority of financial professionals are honorable men and women, a number of forces may conspire to encourage them to act in ways that aren't in your best interests. Therefore, whenever you receive a recommendation for the products listed below, evaluate whether it meets your needs and listen carefully for signs that your advisor isn't really saying the following:

Annuities	"I like it when you buy an annuity with a long surrender schedule because I get paid a huge commission; often times, about 6-7% of your investment."

Illiquid Investments	"Limited partnerships, unit investment trusts, REITs and other alternative investments may be illiquid but that's OK because I get paid a great fee!"
Variable Universal Life Insurance	"Unless you need the life insurance for your beneficiaries or your estate, these policies can be one of the worst investments you can make, but I get paid thousands!"
Proprietary Brokerage Products	"I win trips and sometimes get paid extra for selling certain products. They're often below average products ... but they'll do fine for you."
Past Star Performers	"I really don't know what your fund holds or anything about the fund manager ... but the fund company says they do a great job."
The "Hot Stock"	"Sure, you stand a great chance of losing your money if you buy on rumors but I have a *guaranteed* source of income."

The quick summary of this chapter reads like this:

Take time to understand your investments and how they relate to your strategy. Your overall plan should be well diversified and may utilize some of the products we discussed in this chapter. I simply wanted to give the pros and cons of each investment so you may make an educated decision.

— CHAPTER 6 —

TAX REDUCTION STRATEGIES

When it comes down to it, there are only two ways to improve your financial condition: (1) increase your income; and/or (2) decrease your expenses. In much of this book, we have discussed ways to accomplish the former by making your money work harder for you. However, in this chapter, we're going to discuss a way to accomplish the latter.

In looking to reduce your expenses, the first place to start is with your single biggest expense – **taxes**. If you're like most Americans, over the course of your lifetime, you've spent more money on taxes than you have spent on your home, your kids' college educations, your vacations, or any other single expense. Therefore, reducing your tax liability is the most logical step in reducing your overall expenses.

This is particularly true because it doesn't require you to scale back your standard of living. In fact, it does just the opposite. Reducing your tax liability allows you to increase your standard of living by using those funds to pay for vacations, a new car, or pursue your passions.

Yet, despite this obvious advantage of reducing tax liability, most people pay more in taxes than they have to. But why? There are two main reasons. First, many people are simply unaware of some of the simple tax reduction strategies available to them. After reading this chapter, you won't be one of those people. Second, some people have the mistaken view that paying more in taxes makes them somehow more patriotic. Of course, nothing could be further from the truth.

There are many ways to support this glorious country. Perhaps the best way is to invest your money into the stock and bond markets. By doing so, you provide these companies with capital to produce useful goods and services and provide jobs for their employees. Another way involves investing in local, state, and federal bonds. Your money is used to construct roads and bridges and to provide for ongoing improvements to our public infrastructure. Yet, another way is to donate money to churches and social organizations that feed the hungry or heal the sick. Therefore, when you reduce your tax liability, you don't weaken the country; you simply control how you want your money to help our great country.

Of course, I'm not suggesting that you *evade* paying income taxes that you lawfully owe. You have a legal and ethical obligation to pay the amount of taxes you owe to the government. However, that amount isn't set in stone; it's determined by your financial situation. To the extent that you don't use all of the tax breaks afforded to your particularly financial situation, you're overpaying your taxes.

And what for? In this country, we don't give awards to people who overpay their taxes. We don't throw banquets in their honor, carve their likenesses into Mount Rushmore, or paint their faces on dollar bills. Nor do we have holidays in their honor or name elementary schools after them. Sure, there's nothing wrong with overpaying your taxes, but there's nothing particularly "right" about it either. When most people list the qualities of a good person, overpayment of taxes doesn't even make the list. So you should feel perfectly at ease with the concept of paying your fair share and no more. I'm proud to pay taxes to the United States; However, I could be just as proud to pay half as much!

Types of Taxes

On the local, state, and federal levels, governments impose taxes in a staggering number of ways. City governments issue property taxes on real estate holders. Also, in some instances, there are excise taxes on personal property (e.g., automobiles, equipment, etc.) and sales taxes. Many state governments also have sales and excise taxes. Moreover, most states also have income taxes. Finally, the federal government collects income taxes, social security taxes, capital gains taxes, and estate taxes, just to name a few.

Now the sad truth is that there isn't much you can do to reduce your liability for certain taxes. For instance, if your city or state imposes a car tax, you're pretty much stuck with it. However, the two largest tax liabilities for most retirees are income and capital gains. Fortunately, both income taxes and capital gains can be significantly reduced through careful tax planning.

Rockefeller's Secret

Rockefeller said that one of the surest ways to wealth was to avoid paying taxes on investment earnings. The key is to either have tax-free income or defer your taxes into the future. Currently, there are very few tax-free investments available to investors. In other words, if you invest money and earn a return, the government is going to want its cut sooner or later.

A notable exception to this rule is the interest earned from municipal bonds, which are bonds issued by state and local governments. The federal government doesn't tax the interest earned on these bonds. An exception would be the Alternative Minimum Tax (AMT). In addition, most states won't tax the interest you earn on their bonds. At one time, municipal bonds were available only to the very rich because they are usually issued in denominations of $100,000 or more. However, with the explosion of the mutual fund industry, municipal bond funds are available to investors of all sizes.

Yet, despite the tax benefits of municipal bonds, there are a few drawbacks. For one, municipal bonds pay lower rates of interest than their taxable counterparts. Therefore, as a general rule, only those taxpayers in the higher tax brackets will obtain a net benefit from investing in municipal bonds.

Also, you should note that municipal bonds are **not** risk-free investments. In addition to the normal risks associated with fixed-income securities, such as interest rate risk, municipal bonds are subject to credit risks. City and county governments can (and do) go bankrupt from time to time. In these cases, investors can lose all or a portion of their investment.

On the other side of the coin is the concept of tax deferral. The purpose of tax deferral is to allow you to make use of your money for as long as possible before turning over a portion to Uncle Sam. In essence, you get to earn money on your money and Uncle Sam's money. Not a bad deal! And while this may not seem like such a big deal, it can make a huge difference over time.

For example, let's suppose that you invested $10,000 into a tax-deferred vehicle that appreciates at a rate of 10% per year. After 10 years, your investment would be worth $25,937.42. Let's further assume that your highest marginal tax rate is 37.6%. Upon cashing out of your investment, you will pay taxes on the gain of $15,937.42 at the rate of 37.6%, for a total tax bill of $ $5,976.53. After taxes, you will still have a gain of $9,960.89.

On the other hand, let's suppose that you invested the same $10,000 into an investment where the returns were taxable in the year earned. Let's further assume that you paid the tax by liquidating that portion of your investment equal to the tax bill. In this case, after 10 years of paying taxes annually at the highest marginal rate of 37.6%, your investment would be worth just $18,335.36. As a result, tax deferral over a 10-year period would have resulted in more than $1,500 extra of investment returns.

Of course, over a longer period, the results would even be more pronounced. Over 20 years, the tax-deferred investment would be worth $45,796.87, which is approximately $12,000 more than the value of the immediately taxable investment over the same period. And after 30 years, the difference would be a whopping $41,000, or more than four times the original investment.

Figure 6.1

	Tax Deferred Investment	Immediately Taxable Investment
10 yrs	$19,960.89	$18,335.36
20 yrs	$45,796.87	$33,618.53
30 yrs	$112,808.76	$61,640.79

Figure 6.2

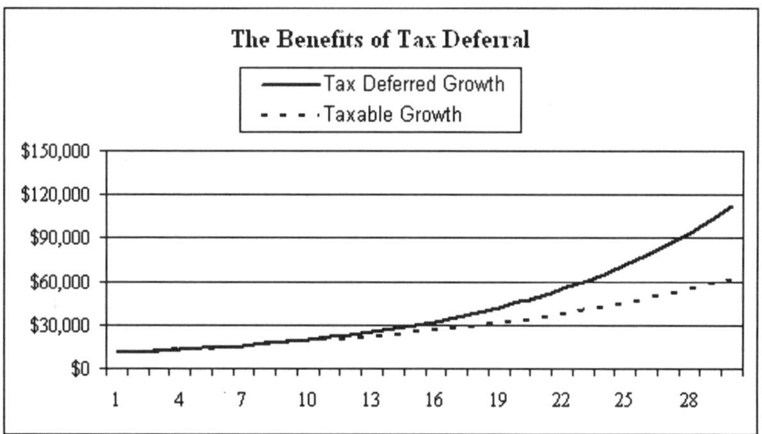

Tax Treatment of Various Investments

Now, that we've discussed the advantages of tax-free and tax-deferred investments, let's take a few moments to review the tax treatment of various investments.

Fixed Income Investments

As a general rule, the interest paid on bonds, notes and CDs is taxable as income each year. Also federal bonds are usually free from state and local taxes but are taxed as income on the federal level. And interest received from bank accounts, CDs, and corporate bonds are taxable as income on both the federal and state levels.

The current taxation of fixed income investments isn't usually a problem because these investments pay interest on a monthly, quarterly or annual basis. As a result, you simply need to set aside a portion of the interest to pay the taxes.

However, this process isn't so straight forward with *zero coupon bonds*.

As the name implies, zero coupon bonds don't pay zero interest until maturity. At maturity, all of the investor's principal and accrued interest is paid to him. As a result, these bonds are issued at a discount to face value. For instance, a $100,000 10-year zero coupon bond with a yield of 5% will be issued at $61,391.33. The holder of such a bond would realize an interest gain of $38,608.67, all payable upon maturity.

Nevertheless, even though the interest won't be paid until maturity, the IRS imputes interest to the bondholder each year. Therefore, each year, a portion of the interest gain will be added to the bondholder's taxable income, even though he hasn't received any cash. This is referred to as "phantom income" and it can lead to some scary situations as the bondholder scrambles to find real cash to pay to the IRS as a result of this paper gain.

Fortunately, in some cases, it's possible to avoid the phantom income. For instance, if you invest in EE savings bonds, you can elect to defer your taxes on interest income until the bond matures (or you otherwise receive cash from selling or redeeming the bond). This is called the cash basis method and allows you to use a portion of your proceeds to satisfy your tax liability as opposed to moving funds from other sources to pay the tax.

Individual Stocks

Your investment return on individual stocks can be taxed in one of two ways. First, you pay ordinary income on any dividends paid to you by the corporation. Secondly, you pay capital gains tax on any realized gain on the value of the stock. Generally, the gain is only realized when you sell the stock.

The tax on corporate dividends has been correctly criticized as a "double tax" since the corporation must first pay income taxes on its profits and then stockholder must pay income taxes on these same profits as they're passed down to her. Yet, despite the efforts of some politicians in recent years to exempt corporate dividends from taxation (or at least, reduce the rate of taxation), as of this writing, corporate dividends are still taxable. This is wrong and you should let your Representative know this!

Realized capital gains are taxed at different rates than dividends, which are taxed as ordinary income. There are two types of capital gains: long-term capital gains and short-term capital gains. Long-term capital gains are those gains realized after holding the stock for more than one year (at least 366 days). Any stock held less than one year is subject to short-term capital gains treatment.

The purpose of this distinction is to encourage investors to hold stock for the long-term. As a result, long-term capital gains rates are much lower than short-term capital gains rate. For instance, at present, the lowest long-term capital gain rate is just 5% for lower-income taxpayers and 15% for all others. In contrast, the maximum rate for short-term capital gains is 35%. This can make a huge difference… make sure you understand how capital gains affect your investments! This can reduce your taxes by 50%!

Mutual Funds

While mutual funds are essential for most individual investors to achieve adequate diversification, they do carry adverse tax consequences because all dividends and capital gains earned in a mutual fund pass straight through the individual holders of the fund. Therefore, mutual funds have all of the disadvantages of owning individual stock, except that the investor has no control over the timing of purchases and sales.

This can be problematic for two reasons. First, it can create a significant amount of phantom income. As a mutual fund investor, you're taxed on dividends and gains, even though those proceeds are often reinvested back into the fund.

Second, you can be taxed on long-term gains that were earned well before you ever joined the fund. For instance, let's suppose you invest in a mutual fund that is holding a stock that has tripled over the last five years. If the fund manager sells the stock on the day after you joined the fund, you'll be taxed for *all* of the gain on that stock over the last five years. As a result, it's possible to join a once high-flying fund, lose money on your investment and still *owe* taxes for gains that accrued before you joined the fund.

It's important to not only explore the past investment performance of the fund but also, the possible capital gains exposure of the fund. Fortunately, some of the mutual fund ranking services like *Morningstar* include a tax analyzer to help you avoid incurring excessive exposure to capital gains. When working with an advisor, make sure you discuss this particular tax topic in depth with him/her. This tip can make the difference between buying a car with money you may have sent to Uncle Sam!

Primary Residence

For tax purposes, your primary residence is taxed just like stock in that you are taxed for any capital gains that occur upon the sale of your primary residence. Of course, you aren't taxed on the appreciation until you actually sell the property. Nevertheless, capital gains on your primary residence can create a rather strange form of phantom income. A **portion** is excluded from **any** taxes and will discuss this in depth in a moment.

The gain on your primary residence is calculated by subtracting the sales price from the purchase price. While this is certainly logical, the amount of your capital gain may be substantially higher than the money you receive at the closing. For instance, let's suppose that you purchased a home 20 years ago for $50,000. Let's further assume that, like many Americans, you've refinanced your home a few times over the years and that your current mortgage balance is $200,000. If you sell your home for $300,000, you will net roughly $100,000 in cash at the closing. Yet, your taxable gain on the property is $250,000 (the difference between the purchase price and the sales price).

At today's historically low long-term capital gains rates (5-15%), you'd have enough money left over to pay the tax. However, you can imagine how this could've created substantial problems in the past when capital gains rates were much higher. To alleviate this problem, the government would allow you to defer your gain if you reinvested in another property within 6 months. In this case, you would assume the cost basis of your original home. Therefore, it wasn't uncommon for people to live in mansions that had a tax cost basis of $50,000 as a couple continually upgraded their homes but kept the cost-basis of their first home for tax purposes.

As you can imagine, this situation could turn tragic during a market downturn. For instance, let's suppose that a couple buys a $1 million home but one year later is forced to sell this home for just $900,000. Let's further assume that after paying off the mortgage and closing costs, the couple walks out of the closing without receiving any cash. Nevertheless, after trading up several times over the years, the couple's cost-basis in this last home is just $50,000, creating a taxable capital gain of $850,000. This could present quite a problem for the couple.

Fortunately, this is no longer a problem thanks to the Taxpayer Relief Act of 1997. Now, a homeowner can exclude up to $250,000 of the capital gain earned from the sale of a primary residence held at least two years. For married couples that file a joint tax return, the exclusion is raised to $500,000. Therefore, for most homeowners, paying capital gains on the sale of a primary residence is no longer an issue. As a retiree, this tax change will allow you to sell the family homestead and travel the world without fear of losing all or most of the appreciation to the tax man. Please consult a qualified tax advisor to review your specific situation!

Income Reduction Strategies

As you know, our personal income tax system is a progressive system. As an American, this is my biggest complaint. We have decided to penalize success. Not only do you get to pay more dollars but a higher percentage. In my opinion, it's not right and it's not fair. The more taxable income you earn, the higher percentage of your income is taxable. And this fact isn't likely to change in the near future. However, the advantage to this type of system is that it can allow you to create disproportionate tax savings by reducing your taxable income.

For instance, let's suppose that after deductions and exemptions, you and your spouse had joint taxable income of $100,000 in 2003. As a married couple filing jointly, your tax liability would be $18,614. On the other hand, let's suppose that you were able to cut your taxable income by 50% to just $50,000. In that case, your tax liability would be just $6,946. As you can see, a 50% decrease in taxable income creates a 63% decrease in tax liability in this case.

Of course, this may not seem like such a good tradeoff if you have to forego "actual" income. After all, it wouldn't make much sense to give up $50,000 in income to save less than $12,000 in taxes. However, it isn't necessary to give up real income to reduce your taxable income. In some cases, your taxable income may be substantially lower (or higher) than your real income depending upon how you "report" your affairs. Therefore, it only makes sense to do a little tax planning so that you can reduce your tax liability as much as possible.

This is particularly true if you're receiving social security. As many of you know, the government has begun taxing social security benefits. Interestingly, the tax only applies to those retirees who were responsible enough to put away adequate funds for their retirement. If a retiree is completely dependent upon social security, her benefits won't likely be taxed. However, if her income (including social security benefits and tax-free municipal bonds) exceeds certain amounts, then up to 85% of her benefits will be taxed at her highest marginal rate.

Many critics of this tax have pointed out that taxing social security benefits is the ultimate form of double taxation. After all, the money that retirees receive from social security is money that was originally withheld from their paychecks as a tax. For the government to levy taxes on the return of the retiree's own money seems unfair to say the least. Nevertheless, this is the law. And for this reason, it's important for all retirees to use any lawful means of reducing their taxable income.

One way to do so is to **time** the purchases and sales of your investments. As a taxpayer, you're taxed on an annual basis for all gains realized during the calendar year. Therefore, in many cases, it will be in your best interest to match gains against losses in a calendar year.

For example, let's suppose that on December 31st, you realize $50,000 of capital gains on a particular stock. The very next trading day, January 2nd of the next year, you have $60,000 of capital losses on another stock. While in just three days you have netted a loss of $10,000, you can't report it this way on tax return. Because the gain occurred in one year and the loss technically occurred in the next year, you can't offset one against the other. As a result, you'll be required to pay capital gains taxes on your gain in the first year. Of course, the next year, you'll be able to claim a capital loss.

However, unless you have other gains that year, you won't be able to claim the *entire* amount of the loss but rather only $3,000 of this loss ($1,500 if you are single). Of course, you will be able to carry forward the remaining $57,000 of the loss into future years. However, unless you can offset this loss against future gains, it will take 20 years before you finally take the entire amount of the loss.

Of course, this situation could have been easily avoided by simply selling the depreciated asset during the same calendar year as the sale of the appreciated asset. In this case, you would have had a capital *loss* in the first year of $10,000, $3,000 of which could have been claimed. Assuming no future gains or losses, you would get the full credit of the deduction within four years and you would have avoided paying any capital gains tax in the first year. As you can see, a little year-end planning can go a long way.

This is particularly true when you consider the disparate rates of taxation on short-term and long-term capital gains. As discussed earlier, the current top rate for long-term capital gains is just 15% while the top rate for short-term capital gains is 35%. So let's assume that the gain in the previous example was a short-term gain and the loss in the previous example was a long-term loss. In this case, the failure to match these transactions in the same year has rather severe adverse consequences.

Assuming you are in the highest tax-bracket, you will have a tax liability of $13,500 on the $50,000 short-term capital gain in the first year. The next year, you will be allowed to take $3,000 of your long-term capital loss, thereby reducing your tax liability by just $450. Even after 20 years of taking this deduction, you will have only received a tax benefit of $9,000. Therefore, you will have paid net taxes of $4,500 on a net *loss* of $10,000.

This is just one of many situations in which it makes sense to match gains against losses in a single calendar year. Another important consideration is in choosing which losses to match against which gains. As a general rule, you should attempt to match short-term gains against long-term losses. Taken individually, long-term losses yield much less of a tax benefit (5-15% of the loss) than short-term gains pose as a tax burden (up to 35% of the loss).

For instance, let's suppose that you have a long-term capital loss of $3,000 in the first year and a corresponding short-term capital gain of $3,000 in the second year. At the top tax bracket, you will receive a tax benefit of just $450 in the first year but incur a tax liability of $1,050 in the second year. However, if these gains and losses were realized in the same calendar year, they would cancel each other out and allow you to avoid the tax loss of $600.

However, in matching up short-term and long-term gains and losses, it's important to realize that similar kinds of gains will be matched up first. In other words, short-term gains will be first matched against short-term losses and long-term gains will be first matched against long-term losses.

To illustrate the significance of this rule, let's suppose that you make three stock sales on December 31st. The first sale results in a long-term loss of $10,000. The second sale results in a short-term gain of $10,000. And the third sale results in a long-term gain of $10,000. Given the matching rules just described, the long-term gain and loss will cancel each other out and you will be left with a short-term gain of $10,000. At the top tax bracket, you would have a tax liability of $3,500.

In this case, it would have been better to delay the long-term gain until January 2nd of following year. That way, the short-term gain would have been matched against the long-term loss. During the next year, you would have had a long-term gain of $10,000. However, given the lower rates for long-term gains, the tax liability would have been just $1,500. Therefore, by delaying the sale just two days, you would have saved $2,000.

As you can see, the timing of sales can make a big difference. That being said, it's important to note that tax consequences shouldn't drive your decision to buy and sell stock. For instance, the desire to set off a long-term loss with a short-term gain shouldn't force you to sell a stock with good long-term prospects. By doing so, you could lose out on much more long-term appreciation than you could ever hope to gain in short-term income tax reduction.

Now, it may be tempting to think that you can have the best of both worlds by selling the stock to accomplish your goal of a matching gain or loss and then repurchasing the stock a few days later. However, the feds are on to this little trick. As a result, the IRS will consider any sale and subsequent purchase within any 30-day period as a "wash sale." As a result, the sale will be ignored and the taxpayer won't be able to use it to claim a capital gain or loss. You must wait 31 days before making your repurchase!

Another way to reduce taxable income is to incur *legitimate* business expenses during each calendar. Now, please understand that I'm not suggesting that you throw away money in far-flung business ventures. Yet, if you currently spend much of your retirement painting seascapes, why not turn your passion into a business by trying to sell your paintings in galleries? This makes sense for at least three reasons.

First, you may find a lucrative second career as an artist. After all, this is how Grandma Moses got started and it worked pretty well for her. Second, why should your beautiful artwork never see the light of day? Your paintings (or poems or novels or photography or whatever it is you have a passion for) could add much needed beauty to the world. Third, you're going to spend the money to pursue your passion anyway. Why not let Uncle Sam underwrite some of the cost?

If you start a business, you can legally claim write-offs for paint, canvasses, the portion of your home used to paint, and even trips you take to do your painting. Once again, you're likely going to spend this money anyway. However, by establishing a business, you can take thousands of dollars off your taxable income.

Of course, you must understand that Uncle Sam is not in the business of paying for your hobbies. As a result, the IRS has established a hobby loss rule. This rule requires that your business turn a profit in three out of every five years in order for you to write off your expenses as business expenses. As a result, most advisors will tell you that you can't take a loss for three straight years because then you won't meet the requirement of showing a profit in three out of five years.

However, this simply isn't true. The hobby loss rule is really more of a safe harbor. In other words, if you turn a profit in three out of five years, then the IRS will give you the benefit of the doubt that you're engaged in a legitimate business. Nevertheless, profitability in the first three years isn't an absolute requirement for a "legitimate" business. There are many million dollar enterprises that didn't earn a profit in their first three years in business. The real true test of whether you can claim losses is if you are truly trying to earn a profit. So long as you're earnestly trying to earn a profit, you're legally entitled to write off the expenses of your business.

For many retirees who start a business, the first question is whether to incorporate or not. In most cases, the answer is "no." In fact, incorporation will negate the tax advantages of incurring business expenses. The important thing to understand is that corporations are separate legal entities. As a result, any expenses incurred by the corporation can't be written off on your personal tax return. Instead, they must be deducted from the corporation's income. If the corporation experiences a loss, then those losses are carried over for future years when the corporation eventually makes money. Yet, in the meantime, these losses will do nothing to reduce your taxable income.

Furthermore, when the corporation begins to turn a profit, it will pay taxes on that income at the corporate income tax rate. Any income distributed to you as a shareholder in the form of dividends will be taxed again. Therefore, not only will you lose the opportunity to take a personal deduction but you'll be double taxed on any income.

The only situation in which it might make sense to form a corporation is when your business could expose you to significant liability. In this case, a corporation can shield you from personal liability. However, there are several instances in which the "corporate veil" can be pierced and creditors can come after your personal assets. Moreover, there is probably a better way to obtain protection from liability by forming a limited liability company (LLC) instead of a corporation.

Most states now allow for the creation of LLCs. LLCs are much like corporations in that they can shield the owners (in LLCs, they are called "members") from liability. Furthermore, LLCs are passed through vehicles for tax purposes. In other words, all gains and losses in a given year pass through to the members. Therefore, if your LLC loses money in the first year, you can deduct that loss (or at least a portion of it) on your personal tax return.

Retirement Plan Rules

As you've likely discovered by now, one of the most effective ways to build funds for retirement is through the use of qualified retirement plans, such as 401(k) plans. One of the chief benefits of these plans is that they allow you to invest pre-tax dollars. Furthermore, your investments grow tax-deferred until withdrawn. When you combine these advantages, the fact that some employers match a portion of the funds that you invest, a qualified retirement plan is the ultimate wealth building vehicle.

In fact, if you're like many retirees, then a large percentage of your retirement assets are in a 401(k) or similar plan. Of course, once you've built up a substantial amount of money in your retirement plan, the question becomes: "How do I get access to this money in the most tax-efficient method possible?" After all, how you access the money has a significant tax impact every year.

One of the requirements of a qualified retirement plan is that you can't withdraw your funds before reaching the age of 59 ½ without incurring a 10% early withdrawal penalty. In addition to paying a 10% penalty for withdrawing funds before this date, you also must pay income taxes on *all* funds withdrawn, not just the investment gain. Since you didn't pay income taxes upon earning the money, you must pay income tax on both the principal and investment earnings.

Furthermore, as significant funds can accrue in these plans, a distribution will often push the taxpayer into the higher tax bracket. As a result, a taxpayer who makes an early withdrawal from a retirement plan can expect to pay almost half of the amount in taxes.

That being said, there are exceptions to the early withdrawal penalty. One such exception is for funds withdrawn to pay for medical expenses, a child's college education and the down payment on the taxpayer's first home (up to $10,000). Nevertheless, it's important to note that even if the early withdrawal penalty doesn't apply, the taxpayer must still pay income tax on all amounts withdrawn.

A final way to avoid the early withdrawal penalty is to take the funds out in substantially equal periodic payments (SEPP) in accordance with the IRS' 72t Distribution Rules. In other words, rather than taking a lump sum distribution before 59 ½ and paying a 10% penalty, you can start taking smaller periodic payments over a number of years. Your financial advisor can help you to determine the amount of these payments in accordance with your choice of the life expectancy method, the amortization method, or the annuity factor method.

One great use for the SEP method of withdrawals is when you go from full-time to part-time work. As you are still earning a portion of your current income, monthly payments from your 401(k) plan can help to bridge the gap until you're eligible for social security.

The SEPP method of avoiding the 10% penalty can even come in handy when you need a large sum of money. For instance, let's suppose that you're 55 years old and you need $30,000 to pay the tuition for grandchild's college education. If you simply withdraw the funds from your 401(k), you will have to withdraw almost $60,000 to cover the ordinary income taxes and the 10% penalty. However, the SEPP option won't completely meet your needs because it will only result in a few hundred dollars per month in income. Nevertheless, the SEPP option can be used in connection with a home equity loan to raise the money. The funds generated from the substantially equal periodic payments could then be used to repay the home equity loan. Of course, another advantage to this option is that the interest paid to the lender is tax deductible in most cases.

Even at age 59 ½, you might not be ready to make withdrawals from your 401(k) plan. Of course, the longer that you're able to allow your 401(k) funds to grow on a tax-deferred basis, the better chance you have of ensuring that these funds last a lifetime. Often times, your participation in a 401(k) plan will be terminated by your retirement, being laid off, or a merger, or sale of your employer. In this case, the funds must be withdrawn from your 401(k). However, the manner in which you withdraw your funds can have a significant tax impact.

In this situation, the best way to keep your money growing tax-deferred is to "roll over" your 401(k) into an individual retirement account (IRA). However, you must be careful about how you accomplish this feat. The best way is to have your 401(k) plan administrator roll your funds directly into an IRA that you establish at a financial institution or reputable brokerage firm. In this way, you avoid some of the pitfalls that can occur during the rollover process.

The first potential pitfall is that you don't roll over your 401(k) funds within 60 days as required by law. If this occurs, then entire amount of your distribution will be immediately taxable as ordinary income. This could leave you with only 60% as much money to continue working on your behalf.

The second potential pitfall is that the 401(k) plan administrator will automatically deduct a 20% withholding. The government requires employers to do this in some situations so that the government gets at least some of "its" money. The problem is that you may wish to rollover the entire amount of your 401(k) account into an IRA. However, once your employer has deducted the withholding percentage, it's too late. Furthermore, if you don't rollover the remaining amount, you will be required to pay the remaining taxes, when you file your taxes.

Of course, there will come a point when the government will want you to withdraw the funds from your IRA so that it can get "its" tax money from you. That point will arrive on April 1st following the year you reach 70 ½ years old. Therefore, if your birthday is before June 30th, then you will turn 70 ½ years old on or before December 31st, and you must start taking distributions by April 1st of the next year. However, if your birthday is on or after July 1st, then you won't turn 70 ½ years old until after January 1st. This means that you have until April 1st of the *next* year to take your first distribution. In this case, you will be more than 71 years old before you have to take your first distribution.

There are three cases in which you can extend the date even further. First of all, unless you are self-employed or your funds are in a regular IRA, you can delay your first distribution so long as you're still employed. In this case, you won't have to make your first distribution until April 1st on the year after you finally retire.

Second, if you previously made a special election to receive distributions under the pre-1984 rules, you're not subject to the age 70 ½ requirement. However, even if this is the case, you may choose to comply with the new rules and begin withdrawing the minimum amount required by these rules. As you will see, this may be advantageous in some situations.

And finally, Roth IRAs aren't subject to this requirement. Even if you are subject to the minimum distribution rules, you should understand that you don't have to withdraw *all* of your money at one time (although you are certainly free to do so). Instead, you must simply withdraw at least the minimum amount required by law. This minimum amount is determined by IRS regulations and it increases each year. Even still, it's possible for a 115 year old person to still retain funds in his IRA. This is a major change from the old rules, which required the retiree to empty his IRA by age 89.

Figure 6.3

Age	Factor	Age	Factor	Age	Factor
70	27.4	86	14.1	102	5.5
71	26.5	87	13.4	103	5.2
72	25.6	88	12.7	104	4.9
73	24.7	89	12.0	105	4.5
74	23.8	90	11.4	106	4.2
75	22.9	91	10.8	107	3.9
76	22.0	92	10.2	108	3.7
77	21.2	93	9.6	109	3.4
78	20.3	94	9.1	110	3.1
79	19.5	95	8.6	111	2.9
80	18.7	96	8.1	112	2.6
81	17.9	97	7.6	113	2.4
82	17.1	98	7.1	114	2.1
83	16.3	99	6.7	115+	1.9
84	15.5	100	6.3		
85	14.8	101	5.9		

**According to IRS Regulations 1.401(a)(9)-9 as of April 17, 2002.*

The above table lists the actuarial factors used by the IRS in determining the minimum distributions for the ages 70 through 115. Each year, the retiree is required to withdraw an amount equal to the balance of the IRA divided by the factor. For instance, a 78-year old retiree with an IRA balance of $300,000 would be required to withdraw $14,778.33, or just under 5% of his total funds, by April 1st.

Under this system, the retiree only gradually needs to start withdrawing funds from his IRA. At age 70, the initial withdrawal represents just 3.6% of the IRA balance. However, each year, this percentage gradually increases to 47% of the balance at the age of 115. Yet, even at this point, the retiree must only withdraw 47% each year, which will allow him to keep funds in the IRA indefinitely. The chart below illustrates the slowly declining balances of an IRA earning a 5% annual return and starting with a balance of $300,000 at age 70.

Figure 6.3

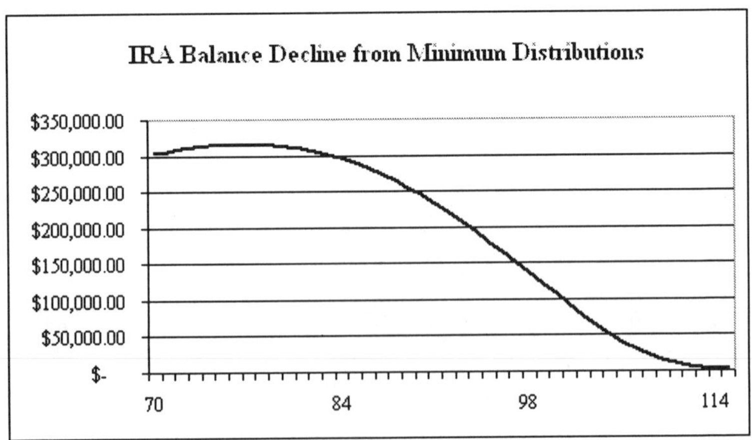

However, the important thing to note here is that while the minimum distribution requirements are not particularly burdensome to follow, there are draconian penalties for failure to comply. If you fail to withdraw the required amount by April 1st, the IRS assesses a penalty of 50% of the amount that should have been withdrawn. In some cases, this penalty could be tens of thousands of dollars. Ouch!

For obvious reasons, you should consult your tax advisor before calculating your minimum distribution. Furthermore, you should consult your tax advisor before implementing any of the strategies discussed in this section. The advice provided herein is merely intended to provide useful information but should in no way be relied upon for investment, legal, or accounting purposes.

— CHAPTER 7 —

LONG-TERM CARE

If you've made it to the point of retirement, then chances are excellent that you were already familiar with many of the concepts we've discussed in this book. You've probably been investing for the last three or four decades. In addition, you may have already put into place some of the tax reduction strategies discussed in the last chapter. However, if you are like most retirees, you've neglected the single biggest risk facing your retirement assets – the expense of long-term care.

If you're currently 65 or older, there's a 40% chance that you'll require long-term medical care at some point in your life.[i] And remember, those are *your* odds for requiring long-term care. If you're married, then the chances that one of you will need long-term care are almost 2 in 3.

You may be thinking, "What's the big deal? We all get sick sooner or later." And while that's certainly true, long-term care should be a concern for every retiree simply because of the cost. The cost of long-term care can range from $3,000-$6,000 per month. Obviously, this type of monthly expenditure can wreak havoc on even the most financially secure couples. This is particularly true if one spouse goes into a nursing home and the other spouse must somehow find a way to pay for long-term care and still pay the mortgage, the car note, the utilities, etc. How do you feel about bankrupting your spouse?

Even worse, the cost of this care is only expected to increase in the future. After all, in a market economy, the biggest determinant of prices is the law of supply and demand. The law states that the greater the demand for a service relative to its supply, the greater the price for that service and vice versa. Well, the demand for long-term care will only increase as 10,000 people turn 59 ½ each day for the next 20 years. Therefore, it's incredibly likely that the price will also increase somewhat dramatically in the future.

The Medicare/Medicaid Myth

Sadly, many retirees don't plan for long-term care because they've bought into the myth that Medicare will take care of these expenses. **This simply isn't true!** First of all, Medicare only kicks in if you've been in a hospital for at least three days and then enter into a skilled nursing center within 30 days of being hospitalized. Even then, Medicare only pays for the first 100 days (and it may only pay a portion of your expenses during this period). When you consider that the average nursing home stay is just less than 3 years, Medicare will only pay a very small portion of your total bill.

You may be thinking, "But hey, isn't that where Medicaid comes into play?" The answer is "yes" but only if you're indigent. Or in other words, you don't have any funds to pay for your own care. If you do have income and assets, then Medicaid will only cover the balance of what you can't afford after going through all of your own assets.

In the past, retirees would often give away their assets to family members just before applying for Medicaid. The theory was "Why spend my children's inheritance on long-term care when the government will pay for it?" There was a certain wisdom in this sentiment. In fact, there was so much wisdom that Congress passed a law in 1993 to make it more difficult for retirees to give away their assets prior to applying for Medicaid. Now, retirees aren't eligible for Medicaid if they've given away financial assets within the last three years. Moreover, I assume since your reading this book, you don't have a goal of becoming a ward of the state. When you qualify for Medicare, you're just that.

Another popular strategy was to establish a Medicaid trust. Retirees would place all of their assets in an irrevocable trust and then claim that they were without assets. In theory, this would make them eligible for Medicaid. However, recently, the government has been clamping down on the use of Medicaid trusts. In some cases, a retiree who establishes such a trust must wait five years before applying for Medicaid.

As you can see, it's becoming more and more difficult to transfer your assets in an effort to get the government to foot the bill for long-term care. Besides, even if you can get Medicaid, you have to ask if you want to. Not all nursing homes accept Medicaid as payment. In fact, just a small minority of nursing homes will accept it and as you can imagine, on average, these aren't the best facilities. In fact, the stories of abuse in some Medicaid facilities are beyond description.

Long-Term Care Insurance

Fortunately, there are other ways to pay your long-term bills other than going on the public dole. One of the best ways to handle the risk of long-term care is to insure against it. You can buy a policy that will pay for all or portion of your expenses if you should ever require long-term care. Of course, the problem for many retirees is that they wait too late to consider buying a policy. By the time, they realize the need for it; they resemble the woman in the following conversation.

Woman: "Hello? Is this Allstate? Well, I'd like to insure my home. Can I do it by phone?"

Insurance Agent: "I'm sorry, ma'am, but I have to see your home first."

Woman: "Then you'd better get over here right away – because it's on fire!"

Needless to say, this woman is going have a difficult time finding a company to insure her home. Likewise, if you wait until you're in poor health or reach your 80s, you will likewise have a difficult time finding an insurer. The best time to buy long-term care is in your 50s. It's possible to obtain adequate coverage as a retiree if you're relatively young and in good health.

In considering any long-term care policy, one of your first concerns should be the financial stability of the insurer. As far as insurance goes, this is a relatively new segment of the industry and it has attracted its share of fly-by-night companies. Since it may be 20 or 30 years before you need to cash in your benefits on this type of policy, it only makes sense to insure with a company that is likely to be around for the long haul. Also, you should look for an insurer with a history of keeping premiums stable. As a general rule, insurers have the right to raise future premiums at any time so it's important to find a company that doesn't exercise this right too liberally.

Another concern should be the elimination period of your policy. The elimination period is the amount of time you must be in a nursing home before you benefits kick in. The elimination period is much like the deductible on your health insurance policy; the longer your elimination period, the lower your premiums. Typically, elimination periods run from 30 to 180 days in length. For many people, 90 days is the best choice for an elimination period since Medicare will take care of the first 100 days of most nursing home stays.

On the other side of the coin is the question of the benefit – how long you will be able to receive benefits. Often, the choices are three years, five years, or a lifetime of benefits. Obviously, the longer the benefit period, the more expensive are the premiums. Given that the average nursing home stay is approximately than three years, many people mistakenly believe that they don't need any more than three years of coverage. However, it's important to remember that the average length of stay is just that; the *average*. It includes people who suffer debilitating strokes and heart attacks and die within days or weeks of entering a nursing home. On the other end of the spectrum are people who live a decade or more in a long-term care facility.

That being said, a three-year benefit term does make sense if you can't afford a longer period. After all, some coverage is better than no coverage. It also makes sense in the case that you've given away all of your assets to qualify for Medicaid. You must remember that even if you are indigent, you don't qualify for Medicaid until at least three years after the gift (in some states it may be longer). Therefore, a long-term care policy with a three-year benefit period may be just the thing to provide you with coverage until you are again eligible for Medicaid.

Now, regardless of the length of your benefits, most benefits are based on a daily benefit amount. Therefore, if the cost of long-term facilities in your area is $3,000 per month, a $100 daily benefit will be sufficient to cover the cost of your stay. Likewise, if the cost is $6,000 in your area, then your daily benefit will need to be $200.

In considering the amount of your daily benefit, you should be sure to take into account other forms of income that will be flowing your way, unless those funds will be required to support your spouse. For example, if you are single and receive $1,200 per month from other sources, you should reduce your daily benefit by $40. Long-term care coverage can be quite expensive so you may want to avoid over insuring.

Some policies are offered with an inflation rider. This rider increases the amount of your daily benefit each year to help fight off the effects of inflation. Unfortunately, in many cases, the inflation rate used by the insurance company is inadequate. While the general rate of inflation has been very low for the last decade, the rate of price increases for nursing home care has risen dramatically. As a result, the minimal protection provided by some inflation riders doesn't justify the increased premium costs.

In addition to determining the amount of the daily benefit, it's important to determine how this amount will be paid. There are two basic types of plans: indemnity plans and reimbursement plans. Indemnity plans pay you a predetermined daily benefit when you become eligible for coverage. On the other hand, under a reimbursement plan, the insurer will reimburse you for any covered expenses you incur up to the maximum daily benefit of your policy.

As a general rule, indemnity plans are superior for two reasons. First reimbursement plans can be frustrating because they require you to keep receipts and submit claim forms to be reimbursed. As the reimbursement process will certainly take weeks, this means that you'll be continually out of pocket for a portion of your expenses. Second, reimbursement plans cap the daily benefit at the *lesser* of your maximum daily benefit or the amount you actually spend. Therefore, if your actual expenses are less than your maximum daily benefit, you don't get to keep the difference although you have higher premiums to acquire this greater level of coverage. Of course, to compensate for these disadvantages, reimbursement plans are generally slightly less expensive than indemnity plans.

In that vain, it's also important to make sure that your policy will pay the daily benefit regardless of whether your stay is covered by any other plan for which you may be eligible. Otherwise, you could find yourself in the middle of a tug-of-war between two insurers as they fight over which must pay for your care.

Another important factor to consider in choosing a policy is when and how you receive benefits. Must you be totally or just partially disabled? Must you first be admitted to a hospital for a certain period of time? If at all possible, you want to find a policy with as little bureaucratic "red tape" as possible. Let's face it. You're going to be spending as much of your retirement as possible living the good life and the last thing you would probably consider is to prematurely check yourself into a nursing home. However, if your time comes when you need to be under the care of others, you don't want to be required to jump through hoops to prove that you're really sick.

Another consideration is what type of care is covered. Are you only eligible for nursing home care? What about home care or assisted living? Home care benefits allow you to live in your current home and have doctors, nurses and other healthcare professionals come to you. Obviously, this type of coverage is more expensive but it can be worth it, particularly if you're married. A home care benefit will allow you to stay home with your spouse rather than being separated should you need ongoing care. As you can imagine, this type of coverage will add to the cost of your premiums but it can be well worth the added expense.

A related consideration is to carefully review the insurer's list of exclusions for coverage. All long-term care policies will list certain situations in which the insurer will **not** honor a claim for benefits. A standard exclusion is for injuries that are intentionally self-inflicted. Therefore, if a person tries to commit suicide, he won't be able to collect long-term care benefits if he is severely injured in the attempt. As you can see, many of the exclusions will be reasonable and will exclude coverage for injuries that result from drug or alcohol abuse or from the commission of a crime.

However, it's important to always read the fine print because some policy exclusions aren't as reasonable or obvious. For instance, some policies won't pay for care if it becomes necessary because of a mental condition like depression or schizophrenia. Even worse, some policies attempt to exclude Alzheimer's disease as such a mental condition. Other policies will attempt to exclude preexisting conditions. For obvious reasons, this is simply unacceptable. After all, the most likely cause of any future disability will be a current health problem.

This is important to remember when applying for your long-term care policy. In most cases, your premium will be based on your past medical history. For this reason, it may be tempting to not disclose certain illnesses or habits like smoking. However, if you leave out this information, you are committing insurance fraud. Not only is insurance fraud a crime but also, it will allow your insurer to deny your claim for benefits. You should disclose *everything* in your application; even those things that your agent says are "no big deal." When in doubt, **disclose**.

In some cases, your disclosures will cause you to be placed in a higher risk category, which will lead to higher premiums. Nevertheless, it's better to pay a higher premium and get your benefits than to try to save a few dollars and lose out on your entire benefit. After all, paying premiums on a policy that you can never collect on is worse than having no policy at all.

Another issue to consider with any long-term care policy is guaranteed renewability. You want to make absolutely sure that your insurer can't simply cancel your coverage down the road. The last thing you want to happen is to pay 20 years into a policy and then have the insurer cancel your policy when you reach 80 and are most likely to need the benefits. At that point, you will have a difficult time obtaining a new policy and even if you do, the new premium will likely be much higher than your original premium.

A final issue to consider is whether your policy will be tax-qualified or nonqualified. Long-term care insurance plans that meet certain conditions allow you to receive two important tax benefits. The first benefit is that you won't have to pay federal income taxes on your daily benefits. The second benefit is that your premiums may be treated as tax deductible medical expenses. Of course, before purchasing any plan, you should consult with your tax, financial, or legal advisor for advice about your particular situation.

In fact, you should have a trusted advisor explain your policy in detail to you. As you can see, there are a great number of variables in choosing a long-term care insurance plan. Therefore, it's important to have someone explain all of the terms and conditions that are ***written*** in your policy. All insurance contracts contain a clause called the integration clause, which states that the terms of your policy are fully set forth in the document and that no other terms will be applied to your policy. **Therefore, the promises of the agent who sold you the policy don't count**. Unless a benefit is written into the policy, it doesn't exist. Likewise, if an exclusion is written into your policy, then it will apply to you even if your agent says that the company never enforces it. This is why it's so important to have a knowledgeable person to help you read through all of the legalities and explain the terms to you.

[i] Source: Terence L. Reed, CFP, *The 8 Biggest Mistakes People Make With Their Finances Before and After Retirement*, p. 57.

— CHAPTER 8 —

DIGNITY AND ESTATE PLANNING

Preparing for the End of the Journey

Up until this point of the book, we've been entirely focused on making the most of your retirement years. After all, that is the real point of retirement, isn't it? You can finally take the time to do all the things you said that you'd do "someday when." Well, "someday when" is here. And that's why we've discussed ways to make your money work hard so you don't have to.

Well, now is the time for us to shift gears and start thinking about the end of the journey. The sad truth is that none of us will make it out of life alive. That being the case, it only makes sense to do some planning with respect to our deaths. The decisions we make today can have a tremendous effect on our dignity during those last days and on the financial and emotional well-being of those we leave behind.

Dignity Planning

The concept behind dignity planning is quite simple. By planning ahead of time, you will be able to maintain your dignity even while mentally or physically incapacitated.

For instance, many retirees derive a certain amount of dignity from being able to support themselves. After all, if you're like most retirees, this is the reason that you saved and invested for decades – to have the sense of dignity that comes from being able to pay your own way.

However, would you still be able to pay your way if you were mentally or physically incapacitated? Who would pay your bills? Who would deposit your social security or pension check? Without some type of power of attorney, the answer is "Nobody." If you were in a coma for three months, your loved ones would be forced to either pay your bills out of their own pockets or forge your name to your checks. Obviously, neither of these options is desirable.

Many retirees prepare for this possibility by executing a durable power of attorney naming another person as their attorney-in-fact. As a result, the attorney-in-fact has power to act on behalf of the principal (the person who grants the power of attorney). The scope of the power is usually spelled out in the document and can be quite broad. For instance, it's typical for attorneys-in-fact to have the power to buy, sell, or lease the principal's property. Attorneys-in-fact also often have the right to make business and investment decisions for the principal, file tax returns, and even file lawsuits on the principal's behalf. In some cases, the attorney-in-fact will even be granted the power to borrow money in the principal's name.

Needless to say, these are significant powers to grant to another person. In most cases, your attorney-in-fact will have the right to do anything with your assets that you could do. After all, this is the point of executing the document in the first place. You want the attorney-in-fact to be able to run your affairs if you're unable to do so.

However, you probably don't want the attorney-in-fact to be able to act while you're still healthy. Many retirees execute a *springable* durable power of attorney. As the name implies, the power of attorney under this document only "springs" into action upon some future event, such as you being certified by a physician as being incompetent to manage your own affairs. However, before that time, the attorney-in-fact will have no power to buy, sell, or borrow in your name.

Needless to say, you should only grant a durable power of attorney to someone in whom you have absolute faith and confidence. In many cases, the most logical choice for the appointment of an attorney-in-fact is your spouse, particularly if you've been married for 30 or 40 years. In that case, it's highly unlikely that your spouse is going to sell your assets and run off to Tahiti the moment you check into a hospital. Another common choice for attorney-in-fact is a retiree's adult child. Have a long discussion with your child and make sure they understand your wishes. Be clear on issues that are important to you. Communication is **critical** to the Power Of Attorney process

A power of attorney is a legal document and as a result, it should be drafted by a licensed attorney experienced in this area of law. In other words, the attorney who handled your workmen's compensation claim may not be the best person to draft your durable power of attorney. After all, you wouldn't consult your podiatrist about a heart problem. The same principle applies in dealing with attorneys.

In addition, although forms of this document exist in stationary stores and on the Internet, it's probably better to still hire an attorney to draft your document. For one, the legal requirements vary from state to state and as a result, the form that you find in the back of a book may not be valid in your state. For instance, one state may require that the power of attorney be signed by one witness while another state may require two witnesses. Second, your particular situation may require a unique approach. For instance, let's suppose that you and your brother run a family business. If you name your spouse as your attorney-in-fact, you may want to exclude certain powers related to the business since your brother may be in a better position to make those decisions. A competent attorney will ask the right questions to make sure that you tailor your durable power of attorney to properly handle your unique situations.

Sometimes, retirees seek to avoid the time and expense of having an attorney draft a durable power of attorney by simply transferring assets into joint ownership with another person, such as an adult child. In that case, if the retiree falls ill, the adult child can take action as a joint owner of the property. While this may seem like the simplest way to deal with the issue of incapacity, it is fraught with pitfalls.

The first pitfall is that there is no such thing as a springing joint tenancy. If you add your adult daughter to your bank account, she becomes an immediate joint tenant. As a result, she can begin making withdrawals even though you are still perfectly healthy. Therefore, unless she is an extremely dependable and loyal person, you could be placing yourself in a very precarious position. Sadly, the news is full of stories about retirees who have fallen victim to the irresponsibility of their adult children.

Nevertheless, even if you have complete faith in your adult child, there are a number of other reasons to avoid putting the property in joint tenancy. For one, once you add another person as joint tenant, that person's creditors may be able to claim the property. Therefore, using the example above, if your daughter owes debts that she can't repay, her creditors can come after *your* joint checking account.

Second, joint tenancy can create a nightmare in the case of an adult child who goes through a divorce. For instance, let's suppose that you add your adult son as a joint tenant of your home so that he will have the power to sell it if you should ever become incapacitated and need to raise funds to pay for long-term care. Let's further suppose that six months later, your daughter-in-law files for a divorce. Guess whose house she may claim as part of the marital assets to be divided? You guessed it! Yours. With the divorce rate in America at close to 50%, this should be reason enough to avoid putting assets in joint tenancy with your adult children.

Third, most forms of joint tenancy involve a right of survivorship. In other words, if one of the joint tenants dies, then the other joint tenant obtains total ownership of the property. So, for example, let's suppose that you have assets in various brokerage accounts worth $1 million and you name your adult son as joint tenant to help you manage these assets. You also have four other children and upon your death, you'd like each child to receive an equal portion of these assets, roughly $200,000. Sadly, by naming one son as a joint tenant, you have prevented this from happening. Upon your death, the brokerage assets will belong solely to the named joint tenant and won't be included as part of your estate (at least for purposes of distribution). Therefore, your four other children will receive none of these assets.

Finally, in some cases, naming a joint tenant to your account will subject you to an immediate gift tax. This will be explained in more detail later in this chapter. However, the bottom line is that you attempt to save a few dollars in legal fees could cost you substantially more in unexpected taxes.

Another part of dignity planning is determining: (1) who will make medical decisions on your behalf; and (2) how far you want medical treatments to go. Obviously, these are very personal decisions. They often involve deeply-held religious and cultural beliefs that are central to your identity as a person. For this reason, some advanced planning is critical. After all, who do you want making these all-important decisions: you and your loved ones or a hospital administrator?

One way to handle this situation is to execute a health care proxy (sometimes called a durable health care power of attorney). This document names another person to make medical decisions on your behalf if you are unable to do so. If you are married, then in most cases, you will name your spouse as your proxy. However, you may want to have a back-up proxy in case you are both incapacitated at the same time due to an automobile accident or other catastrophe.

Many people mistakenly think that they don't need such a document because their spouse will automatically get to make this decision for them. This is not always true. In fact, there was a recent case where a husband was unable to take his wife off life support because of the objections of her parents. In this type of case, a health care proxy would have been helpful in determining who should have the power to make this very difficult decision.

Furthermore, if you aren't married, then a health care proxy is an absolute must. In the absence of a health care proxy, the decisions over your care will be most likely determined by your adult children. However, if your adult children live thousands of miles away, you may want to empower a close friend to be able to act immediately on your behalf. Without a health care proxy, this person will have to sit by powerless while waiting for your children to arrive from out-of-state.

Also, there will be some cases in which you will want to name someone as your health care proxy but you'll want to force them to act in accordance with your wishes. Or, in other words, you will want them to make decisions about your treatment as you would make those decisions if you were able to do so. One way to accomplish this feat is by executing a **living will**.

A living will states your preferences for the kinds of medical treatment you're willing to undergo (or forsake) under certain extreme circumstances. For instance, you can make your wishes known that if you're ever suffering from a terminal disease or irreversible brain damage, you don't wish to be resuscitated or placed on life support.

Many people have a strong aversion to being kept alive in a persistent vegetative state indefinitely. If you're one of these people, then a living will can help to prevent this possibility. It will also prevent your children's inheritance from being exhausted by enormous hospital bills. If you spent a lifetime amassing a fortune for your family, you may not wish to see it spent on feeding tubes and ventilators. This is particularly true if you have a surviving spouse who is dependent upon those funds to live.

Once again, this isn't an area for a do-it-yourself solutions or pre-packaged software. The law is simply too complex and varied to leave this important matter to chance. This is particularly true because there are no second chances with respect to these documents. If your document doesn't accomplish its purpose because it doesn't meet legal requirements, then you won't be in a position to change it. Your fate will be in the hands of others- perhaps they will be loved ones with your best interests at heart or perhaps they will be doctors, hospital administrators, or social workers with other priorities. In either event, where is the dignity in that? Take control and handle any situation on **your** terms.

Estate Planning

In addition to planning for illness, you will also want to plan for your ultimate death. It's important that you make your wishes known about what should happen to your property, your investments, your business, or the raising of your children (or perhaps grandchildren) upon your death. And, obviously, the only time to make that choice is when you are alive.

Sadly, the vast majority of Americans never make such a choice; at least not in writing. As a result, seven out of every 10 Americans die intestate (without a will). If you become one of the seven, then your home state will graciously draft up a will for you, although you may not like it very much. Each state has its own laws of intestate succession. These laws spell out who is to receive your property upon your death.

Now, in fairness, the laws of intestate succession aren't completely unreasonable. For instance, they don't just arbitrarily give your assets to the mailman or the Governor's brother. Instead, they first attempt to pass your assets down to your surviving spouse and children. If you don't have any, then your assets will generally be given to your parents, siblings, and other blood relatives in a determined order of priority. Of course, the drawback here is that they won't be in *your* order of priority.

You may wish to give more or less than the required amount to your spouse. Likewise, you may wish to give different amounts to your children based on their needs or other factors. For example, if you have a child with a disability, you may wish to allocate more of your estate to this child to pay for his or her adult care needs. Sadly, the laws of intestate succession don't take into account these things. Each child receives the same percentage of your estate.

Furthermore, you may wish to make certain bequests. For example, you may wish to pass down the family china to the oldest child in accordance with family tradition. Or you may wish to give your favorite fishing pole to your best friend. Without a written will, there is no way to ensure that your wishes will be carried out.

This is particularly true if your wishes concern the care of a minor child. As a retiree, it's likely that all of your children are adults but an increasing number of retirees are raising their grandchildren. If you are such a retiree, then I suspect it matters to you who would raise your grandchild upon your death. It's only through a will that you can make your wishes known about such an important decision.

In your will, you can also designate an executor to carry out your instructions and represent your estate. Without a will, one of your heirs must petition to the court to represent your estate. Obviously, you don't get to choose who that heir will be.

Now, assuming that you have a will, upon your death, your estate will enter into probate. This is the legal process for settling your will and distributing your property in accordance with your wishes. In the probate process, the judge will first determine if your will meets all of the requirements for a valid will. If not, then your estate will be settled as if you had no will at all. By now, it should go without saying that you should have your will drafted by an attorney knowledgeable in this area of the law.

Assuming your will is valid, the probate process really gets underway. Your heirs and beneficiaries are notified and the executor goes about the process of inventorying and appraising your assets, collecting money due to the estate and paying creditors and taxes. Finally, the assets are distributed to the proper heirs and the estate is closed. The probate process is generally a fair and orderly method of distributing assets but it has two big drawbacks; it's slow and it's expensive.

On average, probate takes between one and two years to complete but in some cases, the process can drag on for several years. This is problematic because your assets will be, in effect, frozen until your estate is probated. For example, your heirs can't do anything with your home because it will be in your name until your will is probated. Likewise, they won't have access to the bank accounts in your name.

As for the expense, probate typically costs anywhere from 3% to 10% of the value of the estate. With large estates, the amounts can be quite staggering. And, of course, this figure assumes that probate goes smoothly. If your executor becomes embroiled in a legal battle with one or more of your heirs, the costs will only increase.

For these reasons, people are often looking for ways to pass assets to their heirs without having those assets pass through probate. One way that people try to avoid probate is through the use of joint tenancy with a right of survivorship. Of course, as we discussed earlier, there are a number of important drawbacks to this form of ownership. Fortunately, there are other ways to avoid probate for all or at least a portion of your assets.

Your bank and brokerage firm may have special forms that allow you to designate a beneficiary for your account upon your death. These beneficiaries won't have any control over your account while you're alive (in fact, they don't even have to know that they are named as a beneficiary). Upon your death, the value of your accounts will immediately be paid to your beneficiary. This distribution will occur without the added time and expense of probate. The same is true with assets held in IRAs, 401(k) plans, annuities, etc. Usually, you are given the right to name a beneficiary. This person will receive the value of these accounts outside of the probate process.

Another way to pass assets to your heirs outside of probate is through life insurance proceeds. All life insurance policies have a beneficiary designation. The death benefit under your policy will be paid immediately to the person(s) listed as your beneficiary, thus avoiding probate. However, if you name your spouse as the beneficiary under a life insurance policy (or bank or retirement account), it's important to list back-up beneficiaries as well. If your spouse dies before you or at the same time, then those assets will be included as part of your estate and subject to probate.

Perhaps, the most powerful way to avoid probate is through the use of living trusts. A trust is a separate legal entity into which you can pour your assets. After the transfer, the trust becomes the legal holder of the assets and therefore, the assets are not considered part of your estate because they don't belong to you. Of course, the beauty of the trust is that although the assets don't technically belong to you, you can retain total control over them. This is one of the most powerful forms of estate planning.

The trust is set up by the grantor and administered by the trustee for the benefit of the beneficiary. In most cases, the grantor, trustee, and beneficiary will all be the same person. For a single person, this means that he will set up the trust and administer the trust for his own benefit. Likewise, for a married couple, this means that they will set up the trust and administer it for their own benefit. So long as the original trustees are alive and well, no other person need be involved.

When one or more of the original grantors dies, then the trust often acts as a will. It determines who will serve as a successor trustee and who will be the new beneficiaries of the trust. The new successor trustee will then administer the trust before the benefit of the new beneficiaries. This administration may involve investing the trust assets and paying out the investment income to beneficiaries or it may involve liquidating the trust and distributing the assets directly to the beneficiaries.

In fact, trusts provide an incredible amount of flexibility in this regard, much more flexibility than can be achieved with wills. The purpose of a will is to provide for the final distribution of assets to the deceased's heirs. However, a trust can spread payments out over a long period of time. In addition, a trust can provide specific restrictions, such as the money can only be used for college expenses.

Despite the enormous power of trusts, many retirees don't take advantage of them. For one, many people fear that they will lose control of the assets once they are transferred into the trust. In most cases, this is simply not true. As trustee, the grantor has complete control over the assets and furthermore, most trusts can be revoked or modified at any time prior to the death or disability of one of the grantors.

Another reason that people fail to have trusts drafted for them is because they mistakenly believe that trusts are only for the very rich. And while certainly the wealthy tend to take advantage of trusts, you don't need an estate worth millions to utilize a trust. Even the smallest of estates can benefit from avoiding probate and gaining the flexibility offered by trusts.

Some advisors recommend that people transfer all of their assets into living trusts. While, theoretically, this may be sound advice, it can be difficult to register all of your assets with the trust. For one, listing *all* of your assets is a considerable chore at which you are unlikely to be successful. Many wills contain a "pour over" provision. This provision basically states that any of your assets not already in the trust will "pour over" into the trust immediately upon your death. Unfortunately, those assets still have to go through probate but at least, they can be distributed according to your trust instructions, which may be more elaborate than your will instructions.

Interestingly, the time and expense of probate is one of the least concerns for the beneficiaries of many estates. A larger concern is the issue of estate taxes. Amazingly, after imposing taxes on every dollar a person owns during his or her life, the federal government has one more tax to throw in at death – the estate tax. The purpose of the estate tax is to prevent wealthy families from passing down their wealth from generation to generation and creating a ruling class. The estate tax was introduced in 1916 to prevent this by imposing a hefty death tax on large estates. In 2002, the top estate tax rate was a whopping 50%.

Recently, the structure of the estate tax rate has undergone a radical transformation. The end result is that the estate tax rates will fall progressively lower each year until 2010 when they will be eliminated in their entirety. However, in 2011, the estate tax rate will be reinstated and go back to 2001 levels unless Congress enacts new legislation before that time, which is likely. Nevertheless, the rates for 2004 are as shown in **Figure 8.1**.

As you can see, the federal estate tax rates can be quite steep. To prevent the estate tax from eating away at the assets

Figure 8.1

Taxable Estate		The Federal Estate	
From	**To**	**Tax Is**	**Of Amount Over**
$ 0	$ 10,000	18%	$ 0
10,000	20,000	$ 1,800 + 20%	10,000
20,000	40,000	3,800 + 22%	20,000
40,000	60,000	8,200 + 24%	40,000
60,000	80,000	13,000 + 26%	60,000
80,000	100,000	18,200 + 28%	80,000
100,000	150,000	23,800 + 30%	100,000
150,000	250,000	38,800 + 32%	150,000
250,000	500,000	70,800 + 34%	250,000
500,000	750,000	155,800 + 37%	500,000
750,000	1,000,000	248,300 + 39%	750,000
1,000,000	1,250,000	345,800 + 41%	1,000,000
1,250,000	1,500,000	448,300 + 43%	1,250,000
1,500,000	2,000,000	555,800 + 45%	1,500,000
2,000,000	Infinity	780,800 + 48%	2,000,000

of smaller estates, the government allows each taxpayer a tax credit to be used against future estate taxes. For 2004, the tax credit was $555,800. As a result, an estate doesn't have to pay the first $555,800 of estate taxes it incurs. Therefore, as a practical matter, only estates with assets greater than $1,500,000 will be subject to the estate tax in 2004. In 2006, the tax credit will increase to exclude all estates valued at less than $2,000,000. This exclusion amount will be raised by $500,000 in each of the following years until 2009.

Figure 8.2

For Decendents Dying During	Top Estate Tax Rate	Applicable Unified Credit	Exemption Equivalent
2004	48%	555,800	1,500,000
2005	47%	555,800	1,500,000
2006	46%	780,800	2,000,000
2007	45%	780,800	2,000,000
2008	45%	780,800	2,000,000
2009	45%	1,455,800	3,500,000
2010	Repealed	N/A	N/A
2011	55%	345,800	1,000,000

In the past, the estate tax drew criticism because of its devastating effects on some families, particular those of farmers and small business persons. The taxes on an estate must be paid within nine months of the taxpayer's death. While no one enjoys paying taxes, the estate tax is manageable if the bulk of its assets are in cash or readily marketable securities, like stocks, mutual funds, and government bonds. In that case, the heirs can simply sell off a portion of their holdings to pay the tax and keep the remainder as an inheritance.

On the other hand, if the bulk of the estate consists of a business or farm, then selling just a portion of the assets becomes more problematic. After all, it can be extremely difficult to sell 45% of a family-run farm. As a result, many families have been forced to sell the family farm or the family business to raise enough funds to pay the estate taxes. In other cases, families have been forced to go into debt to pay the estate taxes. Therefore, if the bulk of your estate consists of a farm, business or other large assets, estate tax planning becomes critical.

Nevertheless, even if your estate consists largely of cash or easily marketable securities, estate tax planning is important. After all, you didn't work hard your entire adult life to leave half of your assets to Uncle Sam. If you're like most retirees, you want your remaining assets to go to your children, grandchildren and favorite charities. Fortunately, there are some things you can do to reduce the bite of estate taxes.

One way to reduce your future estate taxes is to give some of your assets away during your lifetime. Obviously, having fewer assets in your estate at the time of your death will reduce your estate tax bill. Furthermore, you can experience some the joy that comes from giving.

However, please understand that you can't completely avoid the estate tax by giving your assets away doing your lifetime. This is because the federal government imposes a tax on gifts as well. The gift tax is taxed at the same rate as the estate tax and is payable by the person giving the gift.

Nevertheless, not all gifts are taxable. For one, any gift used to pay medical expenses or tuition isn't subject to the tax. Without this exemption, you would have to pay a gift tax for helping your children and grandchildren through college. Second, gifts to your spouse are exempt from taxation. After all, Uncle Sam figures he can just get the money from him or her when they pass the property along to a third person. And finally, gifts to political organizations and charities are exempt from the gift tax.

Also, gifts under a certain value are also exempt from the gift tax. In 2002, the threshold amount was raised to $11,000 and increases with inflation every year after. Married couples are allowed to "double up" on this threshold and give gifts of up to $22,000 without being taxed. This exemption is a powerful tool for some retirees to pass down a portion of their estate to their children tax-free. After all, using this exemption, a married couple with four children could pass down up to $88,000 of their estate to their children each year *tax-free*. While this may not seem like a great amount, it can have a dramatic impact on the amount of estate taxes your heirs will pay upon your death.

For example, let's take the case of Ralph and Rita Retiree.. In 1992, they had a net worth of $2 million. That year, they set up a gifting program whereby they gave $22,000 to each of their four children. Ten years later, in 2002, Ralph and Rita both died. Over the previous ten years, their net worth hadn't changed, except for the amounts they gave to their children ($880,000 in total). Therefore, their final estate was valued at $1,120,000. As the first $1 million is exempt from estate taxes, their heirs were left with a tax bill of just $49,200.00 By giving away a portion of their assets during their lifetimes, Ralph and Rita were able to pass down $880,000 to their children during their lifetimes and an additional $1,070,200 after their deaths for a total of $1,950,200.

Without such a gifting program, their children would have received considerably less. If Ralph and Rita had died in 2002 with an estate valued at $2 million, the estate tax bill would have been $435,000, leaving $1,565,000 for their heirs. This amount is $385,200 less than the amount that was passed down using the gifting program. As you can see, an annual program of small gifts can pay big dividends over the long run.

Of course, this type of gifting isn't feasible in all situations. For instance, the bulk of your assets may be tied up in your home or in an investment portfolio from which you draw income to meet your living expenses. In this case, you may decide that it's best to keep your current assets and let your heirs worry about the estate taxes.

Also, there will be some cases where you will want to make a gift larger than $22,000. For example, you may wish to give an adult child $50,000 to put down as a down payment on a home or to start a business. If a gift exceeds the threshold amount, then the giver is taxed for the difference. For instance, if you and your spouse had given your child a gift of $50,000 in 2002, you would have been taxed on the $28,000 over the threshold amount. The federal gift tax on that amount in 2002 was $5,560.

Interestingly, even if a gift tax is assessed in a particular year, it need not be paid that year. You can use part of your future estate tax credit to offset the tax bill. For instance, in 2002, the unified gift and estate tax credit was $345,800. Therefore, instead of paying the gift tax directly to the government, you can simply deduct $5,560 from your future estate tax credit. In a sense, you are deferring the payment of the tax

However, there are some cases when you wouldn't want to defer the taxes but instead pay them. By paying the taxes upfront, you further reduce the size of your estate and therefore, reduce your future estate tax burden. For instance, let's suppose that Ralph and Rita Retiree have a net worth of $3 million in 2002 and decide to give away $1 million to their only child, Rachel. The gift tax on $1 million in 2002 was $337,220. Ralph and Rita can either use up most of their tax credit to offset the gift tax or they can pay the tax out of their current assets. By paying the taxes out of their current assets, they reduce the value of their holdings to $1,662,780. If Ralph and Rita both died the next year, the estate tax to their heirs would be just $172,495 (after deducting their unused estate tax credit of $345,800), leaving an additional $1,490,285 to be passed down to their heirs.

On the other hand, if Ralph and Rita had used the future estate tax credit to pay the gift taxes, then their estate would have been worth $2 million upon their deaths. The estate tax on a $2 million estate is $780,800. And as Ralph and Rita would've already used up all but $8,580 of the tax credit, the estate tax bill to their heirs would be $772,220. This would leave just $1,227,780 to their heirs, which is $262,505 less than their heirs would have received if Ralph and Rita had paid the tax upfront.

Finally, when giving to your heirs during your lifetime, you should try to avoid giving assets that have built-in capital gains. By doing so, you can deliver to your heirs one of the few tax benefits of death – a step-up in basis. When assets are transferring to your heirs upon your death, they all get a new cost basis of the value of the asset upon your death. When your heirs sell the property, their gain will be taxed as the difference between the sales price of the asset and its value at your death. This is advantageous for a property with large built-in capital gains, which would otherwise have a much lower cost basis equal to the price paid for the asset 10, 20, 30, or even 40 years ago.

To illustrate, let's suppose that you have a $2 million net worth consisting of two chief assets $1 million in cash and $1 million in company stock, for which you paid $100,000. Let's further suppose that you decide to give away half of your net worth prior to your death. Regardless of whether you give away the cash or the stock, you'll be assessed gift taxes of an equal amount. Furthermore, upon your death, your heirs will have to pay the estate taxes on the remaining $1 million of assets.

However, estate taxes aren't the only taxes that you have to worry about. You also have to contend with capital gains taxes. If you give the company stock to your heirs during your lifetime, they will assume your cost basis in the stock. Therefore, when they sell the stock, they will incur significant capital gains since your cost basis was only $100,000. On the other hand, if you pass the stock down to your heirs upon your death, they will benefit from a step-up in basis. For capital gains purposes, their cost basis will be the value of the stock upon your death (approximately $1,000,000). Assuming long-term capital gains rates of 15%, you can save your heirs approximately $135,000 of capital gains taxes by waiting until your death to pass long the company stock.

Of course, the situation is reversed when you're holding property that has significant long-term capital *losses*. In that case, it's advantageous to transfer the property during your lifetime and retain the higher cost basis for the property. For example, let's suppose that you have a cost basis of $100 per share in a stock that is now trading at just $50 per share. If you transfer that stock during your lifetime, the transferee will assume your cost basis of $100 per share. On the other hand, if the stock is transferred to your heirs upon your death, then the new cost basis will be the value of the stock upon your death, which will likely be less than $100 per share. As a result, your heirs won't be able to benefit from a higher cost basis in the stock unless you transfer it while you're alive.

Another way to reduce estate taxes is to not own life insurance in your own name. Many retirees have been told that life insurance proceeds will flow tax-free to their heirs and this is partly true. Your heirs won't pay *income* taxes on the amounts they receive. However, death benefits paid on life insurance policies written in your name are included in your estate for the purposes of estate taxes. This small detail can have a big effect on your heirs.

For example, let's take the case of Randy Retiree. Randy owned a small business valued at $2,000,000 and a home with $500,000 of equity. Randy's family was very tight-knit and as a result, his adult children worked in the business and lived at home with him. Randy decided to take out a life insurance policy that would pay the estate taxes so that his children wouldn't have to sell the business or the home upon his death. He calculated his total assets to be $2,500,000 and, using 2002 estate tax rates, concluded that the taxes on his estate would be $680,000. Therefore, he took out a life insurance policy in his own name for $700,000 and died shortly thereafter.

Unfortunately, Randy didn't realize that his life insurance proceeds would be included in the value of the estate. This increased the value of his estate to $3,200,000, which resulted in estate taxes of $1,030,000. As Randy's children only had $700,000 in life insurance proceeds, they were forced to sell the home in order to pay for the estate taxes. Sadly, Randy could have avoided this situation if he hadn't purchased the policy in his own name. Instead, he could have used an irrevocable life insurance trust (ILIT) to purchase the policy.

Many advisors recommend that all retirees with a significant amount of life insurance should look into establishing an ILIT. The purpose of this trust is to hold all of your life insurance. You can either transfer ownership of existing policies into the ILIT or you can have the ILIT apply for new insurance on your life.

The former method is by far the easiest but it comes with one major drawback – you must survive three years after the transfer for it to be effective for estate tax purposes. If you should die within the three-year period, then the life insurance proceeds would be included in your estate. Obviously, this would defeat the entire purpose of establishing the ILIT in the first place.

On the other hand, if the ILIT applies for the coverage initially, then there is no three-year waiting period. The life insurance benefits won't be considered part of the retiree's estate. Of course, for many retirees, it may be difficult to apply for new coverage after a certain age. Besides, even if the retiree is insurable, chances are excellent that the new premium will be tremendously more expensive than the original policy. The only exception to this situation would be where the retiree had just recently purchased a policy and therefore, replacing that policy with an identical policy in the name of ILIT would be easy.

Perhaps, a simpler alternative to the ILIT is to transfer the ownership of your existing policies to your heirs or have them take out an insurance policy on your life. Interestingly, the three-year waiting period will apply to any transfer of an existing policy into the name of your heirs. However, a new policy isn't subject to the waiting period. Using either of these strategies, you can save on the time and expense of having an irrevocable life insurance trust drafted. Yet, the downside is that you must depend upon your heirs to make the payments. Also, if one of them goes through a divorce, the insurance assets may become part of the property settlement.

Another way to reduce estate taxes is to "double up" on the tax credit given to all taxpayers. As we discussed earlier, each taxpayer receives a credit against future estate taxes owed. Prior to 2002, the credit was just $230,000. In 2002, it rose to $354,800. In 2004, it further increased to $555,800. As a result, the heirs of any estate valued at $1,500,000 or less in 2004 won't have to pay estate taxes. Interestingly, there is a way to double the credit so that estate taxes won't be assessed against any estate with a value less than $3,000,000.

One of the interesting facets about the estate tax is that it doesn't apply to transfers between spouses. You can leave an unlimited amount of assets to your spouse and he or she won't have to pay a dime of estate tax. This unlimited marital deduction was first introduced into the law in 1981. Before that time, there were many cases in which widows were forced to sell their homes and farms to pay the taxes on their husbands' estates. The unlimited marital deduction alleviated this condition and, in effect, allows your surviving spouse to defer payment of estate taxes until his or her death.

However, as attractive as a tax-free transfer might seem, it does carry a major drawback if you have a large estate. The reason is because you waste your estate tax credit by leaving all of your assets to your spouse. After all, using 2004 rates, your tax credit allows you to pass up to $1.5 million to your children without paying estate taxes. However, you only get to take advantage of this credit by passing assets directly to your children. If you leave everything to your spouse, who in turn leaves the assets to your children, then your tax credit is wasted.

To illustrate, let's take the case of Ralph and Rita Retiree. Ralph has a net worth of $3,000,000 and in 2004, he dies leaving all of his assets to Rita. Accordingly, Rita doesn't pay estate taxes on the transfer. The very next year, Rita dies. Her estate is valued at $3,000,000. Thanks to the tax credit, her heirs don't pay estate taxes on the first $1,500,000, but they do pay taxes on the second $1,500,000. These taxes come to $725,000.

Now, let's take a look at what would have happened had Ralph left $1.5 million to his wife and $1.5 million to his heirs. His wife wouldn't have paid estate taxes because she's exempt from them under law. Furthermore, his heirs wouldn't have paid estate taxes because of the tax credit. Upon Rita's death, the heirs would have inherited another $1.5 million.

Together, Ralph and Rita could've passed $3 million to their heirs without paying any estate taxes.

Many married couples lose out on the opportunity to pass large sums of money to their heirs by not taking full advantage of both spouse's tax credit. The way to do this is to leave up to full amount of the tax credit in each spouse's estate. For instance, in 2004, that amount is $1.5 million. In 2006, it will increase to $2 million.

Of course, many retirees fail to do this because they want their spouses to have the full benefit of their assets to live on. Well, there is a way to do just that and still get maximum use of each spouse's tax credit. This can be accomplished by setting up a revocable life trust with an A-B provision. In the trust document, you state that you wish to include the threshold amount in your estate for the year of your death. This amount is to be held in a trust (the Bypass Trust) for the benefit of your ultimate heirs. All other assets flow into your spouse's trust (the Marital Trust) on your death.

Therefore, your spouse would have access to all funds in the Marital Trust. Even more, your spouse would have use of the income earned from funds in the Bypass Trust. Under government regulations, the trustee of a Bypass Trust may use the income generated by the trust assets to support the surviving spouse. Furthermore, each year, the trustee can use up to the greater of 5% or $5,000 of the trust's principal for the support of the surviving spouse. Therefore, a living trust with an A-B provision will allow you and your spouse to "double up" on your tax credit and still provide financial security for the surviving spouse.

Another trust that can be used to reduce estate taxes is a qualified domestic trust for the benefit of a non-U.S. citizen spouse. The unlimited marriage deduction doesn't apply to assets passed down to a non-U.S. citizen spouse. The concern here for the federal government is that these surviving spouses may return to their countries of origin, thereby "cheating" the government out of its share of estate taxes. By establishing a qualified domestic trust to hold the estate assets, you can alleviate the federal government's concern and therefore, use the unlimited marriage deduction.

When establishing this trust, the surviving spouse is designated as the beneficiary. For a trust to qualify for this special tax treatment, at least one of the trustees must be a U.S. citizen. Furthermore, the trustee must have the right to deduct estate taxes from all principal withdrawals. And finally, the trust must comply with IRS Regulations designed to insure payment of the estate taxes upon the surviving spouse's death. Interestingly, this type of trust can be set up after the deceased spouse's death.

Another trust that can help reduce estate taxes is the charitable remainder annuity trust. In this type of trust, a charity is named as the ultimate beneficiary upon the death of the grantors (you and your spouse). However, in the meantime, you and your spouse can live off the income generated by assets in the trust. This can be the perfect vehicle for retirees who own non-income producing assets with huge built-in capital gains.

For instance, let's suppose that Ralph and Rita Retiree own a vacation home worth $1,000,000, for which they paid $100,000 several years ago. Let's further suppose that Ralph and Rita would like to sell this property and reinvest the proceeds in bonds in order to obtain some additional income. Of course, they could always sell the home for $1,000,000 and invest the proceeds. The only problem is that they will first have to pay capital gains taxes of $135,000 on the $900,000 of profit from the house. As a result, instead of having $1,000,000 to invest in bonds, they will only have $865,000 to invest.

In this case, a charitable remainder annuity trust can be used to avoid the capital gains tax and have the entire $1,000,000 flow directly into investments for Ralph and Rita's benefit. Ralph and Rita would simply need to establish the trust and transfer the vacation home into the trust. The sale of the home by the trust would be exempt from capital gains taxes because the trust was established for a charitable intent. Finally, the trust could be drafted to pay Ralph and Rita all of the income generated by the reinvested funds.

By avoiding the capital gains tax, the trust would have more funds to invest and as a result, Ralph and Rita would earn more income. Furthermore, they would be entitled to a substantial tax deduction for their gift to the charity. The only "losers" in this situation would be Ralph and Rita's heirs, who would lose out on inheriting the home. However, there is a way to make it up to them.

Ralph and Rita could use a portion of their annual income from the trust to fund insurance policies on their lives. The insurance policy would be issued in the name of an ILIT created for this purpose. As a result, upon their deaths, their heirs would receive the death benefit free of estate taxes. In this way, everybody wins (except the IRS).

Legal counsel should be consulted regarding your specific situation. The advice and illustrations provided in this section are merely intended to provide useful information but should in no way be relied upon for investment, legal, or accounting purposes.

CHAPTER 9

YOUR PERSONAL CFO
Finding Your Very Own Tour Guide

In this book, we've discussed stocks, bonds, mutual funds, annuities, REITs, IRAs, life insurance, long-term care insurance, health care proxies, durable powers of attorney, wills, trusts, estate taxes and many of the other building blocks of designing a Financial Life Plan for your retirement years. After reading all of this, you may be slightly overwhelmed. After all, this is a lot for any person to think about, let alone act upon. Yet, action is required for you to get the most out of your retirement years.

Contrary to popular opinion, knowledge is <u>not</u> power. Knowledge is only *potential* power. Putting your knowledge to work is where the true power lies. To help you in this regard, you might want to consider hiring a personal Chief Financial Officer. If your money is going to be working for you during retirement, why not treat it like an employee? Why not hire someone to manage your money and make sure that it's not showing up late and leaving early each day?

This is particularly true if you're relatively new to the area of money management. If you're like many retirees, you've been quite successful at amassing large sums of money through regular contributions to a company-sponsored pension or 401(k) plan. However, as we discussed, retirement investing is quite different from accumulation investing. Therefore, you may want to consider hiring a professional to handle this part of your financial life. After all, if you make a mistake, you won't get a second chance to fix it.

Furthermore, even if you're a financial wizard, you may still wish to enlist the aid of a professional. After all, your retirement should be a time when you spend it doing all the things you never had the time to do during your working years. Do you really want to spend your retirement watching a stock ticker or anxiously awaiting the latest statement by the Federal Reserve Board? Why not hire someone while you paint seascapes, golf in Alaska, drive across the U.S. in an RV, or whatever it is that you'd really like to do?

Besides, being your financial coach is one of the primary benefits of hiring an investment professional. The purpose of a coach is to give you feedback that will enable you to maximize your performance. A good coach does this by evaluating your performance and then giving you just a few tips to take your "game" to the next level. This can be extremely valuable.

Perhaps, this is why most top performers have coaches. For example, although Tiger Woods is arguably the greatest golfer on the planet, he still hires a coach to help him get better. The same applies for most of the other top professional athletes. It also applies to corporate executives, many of whom employ business coaches to help them to constantly improve. Therefore, even if you enjoy the day-to-day aspects of managing your money, a coach can help you to improve your investment returns and accomplish other important goals, such as income and estate tax reduction.

If you decide to hire a personal CFO, then you will obviously want to be extremely careful in choosing the right professional for you. You're going to be depending upon this person for some of the most important advice you will ever receive. For this reason, it's important to make sure that your personal CFO has the required knowledge and experience to help you make the most out of your retirement assets. Furthermore, your personal CFO must have your best interests at heart. Below are eight questions you should ask when filling the position.

1. How long have you been in the investment business?

There is a learning curve associated with any skill. Financial management is no different. People new to the profession will invariably make mistakes. It's part of the process. However, they don't have to make these mistakes with *your* money. Once again, you can't afford to lose a chunk of your retirement assets because of a "rookie" mistake. For this reason, you should be looking for an investment professional with at least 10 years of investment management experience.

On the other side of the coin, you probably don't want to choose an advisor who is nearing retirement himself. After all, you could be retired for a very long time. If you want to establish a long-term relationship with your personal CFO, then you want to make sure that he's still going to be in the business 10 or 20 years down the road.

Furthermore, the advisor's experience should be in dealing with people just like you. Someone who has spent the last 25 years managing billions of dollars of university endowment funds doesn't have the right experience for you. Universities don't have long-term care and estate planning issues. Therefore, while this person may have a wealth of general investment experience, you would be better suited to find a personal CFO experienced in dealing with retirees and the particular issues affecting them.

2. Do you have any professional designations?

The investment business is a fairly well-regulated industry. Most advisors are required to pass one or more tests to ensure their basic understanding of investments. Yet, I suspect that you want someone who understands more than just the basics. You want an expert. In fact, you *deserve* an expert.

Fortunately, there is a way to determine whether your prospective advisor is truly an expert – by their designations. Industry groups like the Society of Certified Senior Advisors issue designations to those professionals who have completed the required courses and demonstrated the experience and ability necessary to be seen as leaders in their fields. Some of the designations you should look for in a prospective CFO are Certified Senior Advisor (CSA), Registered Financial Planner (RFP), Certified Financial Planner (CFP), Registered Financial Consultant (RFC), Certified in Long-Term Care (CLTC), Graduate Estate Planning Consultant (GEPC), Chartered Retirement Planning Counselor, and Accredited Estate Planner Designation (AEP). Look for professionals that have college degrees preferably in finance or accounting and graduate degrees with an MBA is a plus.

Of course, a professional designation is no guarantee of the advisor's true level of expertise. However, a designation does demonstrate that the professional is serious enough about this particular area of investments that she went through the time and expense of achieving the designation. All things being equal, someone with a designation is likely to be more knowledgeable than someone who simply passed a state mandated exam several years ago.

3. What is your investment philosophy, vision, and mission statement?

Remember, it's not so important that you find the "right" investment advisor as it is that you find the right investment advisor for *you*. Your personal CFO should share your investment philosophy and vision. After all, you will be putting him in charge of *your* money. The last thing you want to do is to lose sleep at night worrying about what "crazy scheme" your advisor hasn't gotten you into this week. The purpose of your retirement is taking a well-deserved rest. If you wanted to deal with stress and tension, you would have been better off staying at your old job and earning a nice paycheck.

Likewise, your advisor should have a mission statement. A mission statement is important for two reasons. First, it articulates the goals and objectives of the advisor and her organization. Obviously, the mission statement should reflect that the advisor is first and foremost committed to helping you meet your objectives. Second, and perhaps more importantly, a mission statement serves as a compass for the advisor. Sometimes, the world of investing can get a little disorientating for all of us. Markets fluctuate, the economy goes through cycles, new products are introduced, you name it. Without a mission statement (or a compass), an advisor is like a ship without a rudder. He is simply bobbing along from one opportunity to the next, never really making any progress towards a destination.

Of course, in some cases, an investment professional will work for a large financial services firm which has spent considerable time and expense in developing a very impressive investment philosophy, vision, and mission statement. In most cases, the firm will produce expensive brochures to explain these principles. When you ask about them, your prospective CFO may simply pass the brochure across the table to you to read.

However, if at all possible, you want to hear the words come directly from the advisor. After all, if you choose to employ this individual, you won't necessarily be receiving advice from his firm but rather directly from him. For this reason, it's important to know that the advisor has internalized the firm's guiding principles.

4. Do you work for a firm that offers both proprietary and non-proprietary investments?

Obviously, if your advisors works for a firm that only offers proprietary investments, your options are going to be quite limited in working with this person. For this reason, you'll want to make sure that the advisor's firm can meet all of your needs – stocks, bonds, mutual funds, annuities, life insurance, long-term care insurance, etc. And even if this is the case, you should still give some thought about tying yourself exclusively to one firm. Remember, regardless of the options available out in the market, this advisor can only offer one line of products, which may not be the best products for you in all situations.

5. How are you compensated (fees, commissions, both)?

In considering working with an investment professional, it's important to understand how he is paid. Let's face it. Investment professionals are people too. We need to eat, pay our mortgages, and send our kids to college like anyone else. Therefore, compensation is a necessary part of the advisor-client relationship. The key is to determine if compensation issues will be driving your CFO's investment advice.

For instance, if your advisor is paid solely on commission, your advisor may have an incentive to steer you towards high-commission products that may not be in your best interest. On the other hand, if your advisor is paid a flat annual retainer to provide investment advice, there is little fear that he will intentionally steer you into unsuitable investments. On the other hand, your advisor may not have the greatest incentive to spend much time and effort reviewing your situation on a regular basis because his compensation is the same whether he meets with you once a year or once a month.

Perhaps, the ideal compensation structure is one where the advisor is paid a fee equal to a percentage of your assets under management each year. As a result, the better you do, the better the advisor does. You and your advisor have the same objective – maximization of your assets.

Of course, please understand that I'm not suggesting that this fee structure is the only way to do business with your advisor. If you find the right advisor, you should feel free to work with him on commission basis, a fee basis or a combination of the above. Nevertheless, it's important to always be mindful of how your advisor is being paid in evaluating new investment opportunities proposed by your CFO.

6. Have you had any complaints filed against you?

This may be a difficult question to ask someone but it's important because trouble travels in packs. An unscrupulous financial advisor won't just cheat one person but several. As a result, these people are often easy to spot by the long line of unsatisfied former clients they leave behind. Obviously, the warning lights should go off if an advisor informs you that she has been the subject of more than one or two complaints.

Sadly, if you come across a really bad apple, you might not get an honest answer to this question. For that reason, you may want to check with your state's licensing authority about this person's history. I suggest all investors visit the NASD's licenses site. Here you can do a back ground check on your broker. And finally, if you have *any* doubts about an advisor's ethics, err on the side of caution and take your business elsewhere.

7. Do you have three client references you can give me?

The best information about an investment advisor will come from his existing clients. Therefore, please feel free to ask for references. A sound professional should be able to give you many more than three references immediately. If he is unable or unwilling to do so, run!

And, by all means, follow up with the references provided to you. Of course, in doing so, you should realize that these are likely to be the advisor's best clients. After all, he wouldn't have given you a reference for someone unless he was sure that they'd say good things about him. Therefore, it's meaningless to ask these people generic questions like "Are you satisfied with him as your advisor?"

Instead, you should ask pointed questions about the advisor's working style to determine if the two of you will make a good fit. Ask questions like "How often do you speak to him? Do you receive regular updates about the status of your investments? How often do you get together to review your plans?" From the answers to these questions, you'll be able to predict in advance the type of working relationship you will have with your future CFO.

Trust Your Gut

The questions listed above are intended to help you assess any candidate for the position of personal CFO. Yet, they aren't meant to replace your gut instincts. In many cases, this is the most reliable assessment tool available to you. Your instincts have likely served you well over an entire lifetime. They told you how to marry, what house to buy, what job to take, etc. So don't discount what your gut tells you about a person, particularly if it's negative.

For instance, did you get the feeling that the advisor was more interested in selling you a particular product than looking out for your overall interests? You can usually tell this by replaying the initial consultation in your head. Did the advisor really try to learn about your particular situation or did she just launch into a sales pitch about her firm's latest annuity product?

As a general rule, the initial consultation should be devoted exclusively to learning about your objectives and the advisor's credentials and investment philosophy. For this reason, the advisor should spend most of his time asking detailed questions about your situation. What do you want to do with your retirement? What have you done up until now? What's important to you? What are your current sources of income? Do you have long-term care insurance? What type of estate planning have you done? And the list goes on and on. The point is that the advisor should be learning about your *total* financial situation before presenting any particular solutions. In fact, many professionals will refrain from making *any* recommendations during the first client meeting.

Another thing to consider is the advisor's candor. Do you feel that you received honest *and complete* answers to your questions about the advisor's credentials and practice? Trust is essential to a successful relationship with your new CFO. You will disclose some of the most personal details of your life to this individual and in turn, rely on their advice to protect your retirement assets for you and your family. If you have any doubts about the person's trustworthiness, you should move on to the next CFO candidate.

Working With Your CFO

Once you've chosen a CFO, you will get started on creating (or modifying) your Financial Life Plan. In doing so, you may transfer some of your assets to new investments. Likewise, you might buy additional insurance coverage or invest in annuities. Also, your CFO may refer you to an attorney to draft up one or more trusts for tax purposes.

However, once these initial steps are completed, your relationship isn't over; it's just beginning. Implementing a Financial Life Plan isn't an <u>event</u>; it's an ongoing <u>process</u>. After all, things change. Your personal situation may change. The markets may change. And certainly, the laws will change. For these reasons, you should schedule regular meetings with your CFO, just as you would with your physician. In addition, your CFO should report to you on a quarterly basis. After all, the owners of public companies require their CFOs to report to them quarterly. As the owner of your company, your CFO should do the same.

Of course, you shouldn't feel that you have to wait until the end of the quarter or the end of the year to meet or talk with your CFO. In fact, you should call your CFO whenever there is a significant change in your personal situation. For instance, if one of your grandchildren comes to live with you, this is something your CFO should know about. After all, you may want to change your will and estate plan to provide for special care for this child until he or she becomes an adult.

Likewise, you should probably consult your CFO *before* engaging in any major transaction, such as buying or selling real estate. Your CFO could save you hundreds of thousands of dollars in taxes by helping you to structure the transaction in a tax advantageous manner.

If you decide to hire a CFO, make sure you get the *full* benefit of her vast years of experience. But remember, your CFO can only advise you on situations about which you make her aware. Therefore, never hesitate to get your CFO's advice about any major financial decision. By doing so, you will get the best results from her, freeing you to do what you should be doing – enjoying your retirement.

Summary

Well, we've covered a lot in a short period of time! You're now on your way to achieving the lifestyle you've envisioned for the last 30 plus years. Again, congratulations. You deserve this time and I am going to give you several ideas that you may use to help construct your Financial Life Plan. I am also going to give you examples of what my firm, Lamkin Wealth Management, utilizes for our clients. As you choose your advisor, it can be utilized as a baseline comparison to ensure you are dealing with a professional. I will also include a sample plan, work-book, and branding brochure. This should give you the feel of the materials that should be used in your Financial Life Plan. And finally, I am going to give you 10 quick areas that your plan should encompass and that your advisor should address.

Your Financial Life Plan should address or include each of the following:

1.) Independent Advice - Does your advisor work for a firm that can offer independent and unbiased advice?

2.) Asset Allocation Strategy - Have you or your advisor developed an asset allocation strategy that helps you achieve your lifestyle with acceptable risk levels?

3.) Money Manager Strategy - Have you or your advisor researched the money managers of each investment and looked at their methods of managing money, risk profile, and past performance?

4.) Retirement Projection Strategy - Have you or your advisor developed your retirement budget to achieve your desired lifestyle and reviewed your retirement projection strategy to see if your nest egg will last?

5.) Retirement Distribution Strategy - Have you or your advisor developed a distribution strategy that gives you the greatest chance of not outliving your money?

6.) Income Tax Strategy - Have you or your advisor reviewed your FLP with a qualified tax professional to reduce your taxes and ensure that you are utilizing the latest techniques for tax reduction?

7.) Dignity/Estate Planning - Have you met with a qualified estate planner to discuss your health care and durable power of attorneys, revocable living trust, and/or will? Do your relatives understand your wishes?

8.) Long Term Care - This works hand in hand with the latter. However, Long Term Care should be specifically discussed as it's one of the biggest risk you face.

9.) Financial Life Plan - Do you have a summary document or written Financial Life Plan that addresses your concerns and gives you a blueprint to track your plan?

10.) Review Process - Schedule periodic reviews to continually monitor and adjust your plan as needed. You and your needs will change and your plan should be built understanding the need for change.

In the following pages, I am going to provide you with example materials. These are examples not to be used for your specific situation. These are for illustrative purposes and not specific recommendations.

1. Example of our Confidential Personal and Financial profile
2. My biography and credentials
3. Introductory Brochure for Lamkin Wealth Management
4. Sample Financial Plan – THIS IS NOT A COMPLETE FINANCIAL LIFE PLAN. This is an example of areas that the financial component should address.

That's it, my friend! You're now on your way to a rewarding "retirement" or lifestyle change as I like to call it! Build it and review it frequently and you'll give yourself the best chance for living life on your terms.

May God continue to bless you and your family and Thank You for allowing me to be a part of your success.

Confidential Personal & Financial Profile

Vision

To enhance our clients lives by providing the blueprint to achieve their goals, live their dreams, and enrich the world through their legacy.

Mission

To enrich our clients' lives by developing their personal blue-print that allows each client to seek true wealth. By providing providing proactive wealth solutions, we anticipate needs before they arise and help our clients saty in control of their financial future.

5151 Jefferson Blvd., Ste. 100
Louisville, KY 40219
Office: (502) 961-6550
Fax: (502) 961-6389
E-mail: mark.lamkin@lpl.com
www.marktlamkin.com

Providing world class "wealth-care" since 1991

Confidential Personal Profile

This comprehensive, personal financial planning summary is designed to help you take inventory and assign realistic values to your personal assets and liabilities. It is the essential first step in organizing a sensible financial plan for your future.

Family Information:

____
Your Name Nickname

____
Age Birthdate Social Security #

____
Spouse's name Nickname

____
Age Birthdate Social Security #

____
Residence Address City State Zip Code

____
Mailing Address City State Zip Code

____
Home Phone # Fax # E-mail Address

____
Referred by ❑ Client Name ❑ TV ❑ Radio ❑ Print

Children's Names & Ages:

1) ____________________ 2)____________________

3) ____________________ 4)____________________

5) ____________________ 6)____________________

Occupation:

Your Job title Employer (last, if retired)

# of Years Work Phone # Retirement Date

Spouse's Job title Employer (last, if retired)

# of years Work Phone # Retirement Date

Advisors:

Do you have a preference or a commitment to this advisor?

Financial Advisor's name ❑ Yes ❑ No

Firm Name City/State

Attorney's Name ❑ Yes ❑ No

Firm Name City/State

Accountant's Name ❑ Yes ❑ No

Firm Name City/State

Insurance Agent's Name ❑ Yes ❑ No

Firm Name City/State

Stockbroker's Name ❑ Yes ❑ No

Firm Name City/State

Financial Life Planning Questionnaire

Born ______________________________

Early Years ______________________________

Education ______________________________

Work ______________________________

Today ______________________________

How long have you and your spouse been together and how did you meet?

____

____

____

____

____

What is your earliest memory of money?

____

____

____

____

Are there events happening in your life that concern you?

____

____

____

____

Why are you here?

____

____

____

____

____

What would you like to accomplish by working with us?

____

____

____

____

____

How did 9/11 change your views about money?

____

____

____

____

____

Is money a means or an end for you?

____

____

____

____

____

Are your retired...If so, where did you retire from?

____

____

____

Do you view yourself as retired or retiring or simply changing your lifestyle? How will you support it?

____

____

____

____

____

____

Other than your home, what has been your best and worst investment?

____

____

____

____

____

____

Have you had any experiences with other Financial Planners you'd like to share with me?

____

____

____

____

____

____

How did you accumulate what you have today?

____

____

____

____

____

What are some of the events in your life that could affect your plan?

What would you do if you had all the money you needed?

Are there investments that go against your principles?

Does anyone help you make financial decisions?

What are your biggest fears about retirement?

____

____

____

____

____

What are you looking forward to the most about retirements?

____

____

____

____

____

What are the top 3 things you want to accomplish in the next 5 years?

____

____

____

____

____

What do you like and dislike about your current advisor?

____

____

____

____

____

What would it take for us to become your personal "Chief Financial Officer"?

Concerns & Objectives

General:

	Yes	No	Uncertain
Are you anticipating any major lifestyle change? (i.e., marriage, divorce, retirment, moving, etc.)	❑	❑	❑
If so, what changes are you expecting?	______________		
Are you comfortable with your current cash flow?	❑	❑	❑
Do you anticipate any significant changes in your cash flow?	❑	❑	❑
Do you anticipate any major expenditures in the near future?	❑	❑	❑
If so, what expenditures are you expecting?	______________		

Retirement Planning:

At what age do you expect to retire? ________

At what age would you like to be able to retire? ________

What minimum income will you need (in today's dollars)? ________

If you plan on working after retirement, estimate you expected income: ________

Are you contributing to an IRA? ❑ Yes ❑ No

Are you covered by any company retirement plans? ❑ Yes ❑ No

Type of company pension plan? ________________________

Protection:

	Yes	No	Uncertain
Do you have any potential health problems?	❑	❑	❑
Do you have adequate medical coverage?	❑	❑	❑

	Yes	No	Uncertain
Do you have adequate disability coverage?	❑	❑	❑
Do you have adequate personal liability coverage? Amount? ___________	❑	❑	❑
Do you have enough life insurance?	❑	❑	❑
Do you have an emergency fund (money set aside in savings)?	❑	❑	❑

Estate Planning:

Do you have updated/adquate wills?	❑	❑	❑
Have you established any trusts?	❑	❑	❑
Are you the beneficiary of any trusts?	❑	❑	❑
Will you be receiving a significant inheritance?	❑	❑	❑
Have you adequately considered estate taxes?	❑	❑	❑
Have you provided adquate estate liquidity for your heirs?	❑	❑	❑
Is proper titling a concern?	❑	❑	❑
Do you have long-term care coverages?	❑	❑	❑

Concerns:

Please list any concerns you may have: ____________________

____

____

____

____

Risk Profile

If separate accounts are used, please use supplemental profile.

Please check the appropriate response for each question.

1 What is your age? ______ Your spouses's age ______

2. How much investing experience do you have with stocks or stock mutual funds?

❑ None
❑ A little
❑ Some
❑ A fair amount
❑ A great deal

3. How much investing experience do you have with bonds or bond mutual funds?

❑ None
❑ A little
❑ Some
❑ A fair amount
❑ A great deal

4. What is your investment goal?

❑ Retirement
❑ More current income
❑ Saving for major purchase
❑ Other ____________________

5. How many years do you have until retirement?

❑ Already retired
❑ 5 years or less
❑ 5 to 10
❑ More than 10 years

6. What do you expect to be your next major expenditure?

   ❑ Buying a house
   ❑ Providing for retirement
   ❑ Paying for a college Education
   ❑ Capitalizing a new business
   ❑ Other

7. How many years until this expense is incurred?

   ❑ 5 years or less ❑ 5 to 10 years
   ❑ More than 10 years

8. What are your major objectives for your investments?

   ❑ Current and future income
   ❑ Preserving capital
   ❑ Building wealth for heirs
   ❑ Keeping ahead of inflation
   ❑ Increasing returns

9. When do you expect to use the bulk of the money you are accumulating in your investments?

   ❑ At any time now ❑ In 1 to 5 years
   ❑ In 6 to 10 years ❑ In 11-20 years from now

10. Over the next several years, do you expect your household annual income to:

    ❑ Stay about the same ❑ Decrease moderately
    ❑ Grow moderately ❑ Decrease substantially
    ❑ Grow substantially

11. I am expecting an inheritance of approximately $______________ in:

    - ❑ 0 to 5 years
    - ❑ 5 to 10 years
    - ❑ 10 to 15 years
    - ❑ More than 15 years

12. Due to a general market correction, one of your investments loses 25% of its value a short time after you buy it. What do you do?

    - ❑ Sell the investment so you won't have to worry if it will continue to decline
    - ❑ Hold on to it and wait for it to climb back up and then sell it
    - ❑ Hold on to it
    - ❑ Buy more of the same investment at the new low price

13. Some people need their investment program to generate current income to meet on-going needs. This typically tilts the investment program towards bonds and dividend paying stocks. How accurately does this describe your objectives?

    - ❑ Very accurate
    - ❑ Moderately accurate
    - ❑ Slightly accurate
    - ❑ Not accurate at all

14. You have just reached the $10,000 plateau on a TV game show. Now you must choose between quitting with the $10,000 in hand or betting the entire $10,000 on one of the three scenarios below. Which do you choose?

    - ❑ Take the money and run
    - ❑ A 50% chance of winning $50,000
    - ❑ A 20% chance of winning $75,000
    - ❑ A 5% chance of winning $100,000

15. How large of a temporary decline in your portfolio are you willing to accept before changing your investment strategy, assuming you start with $100,000?

- ❑ 10% decline (portfolio value is $90,000)
- ❑ 15% decline (portfolio value is $85,000)
- ❑ 20% decline (portfolio value is $80,000)
- ❑ 25% decline or greater (portfolio value is $75,000 or less)
- ❑ 50% decline or greater (portfolio value is $50,000 or less)

16. By what percentage do you expect your portfolio to grow annually over the long term, 10+ years?

- ❑ 6% - 8%
- ❑ 8% - 10%
- ❑ 10% - 12%
- ❑ 12% - 14%
- ❑ 14% - 16%
- ❑ More than 16%

____

Signature

____

Print Name

____

Date

Family Assets

Investment (Non-retirement)

$100,000	-	$250,000	❑
$250,001	-	$500,000	❑
$500,001	-	$1,000,000	❑
$1,000,001	-	$5,000,000	❑
$5,000,001	+		❑

Retirement Plan (IRA, 401-k)

$100,000	-	$250,000	❑
$250,001	-	$500,000	❑
$500,001	-	$1,000,000	❑
$1,000,001	-	$5,000,000	❑
$5,000,001	+		❑

Business

$100,000	-	$250,000	❑
$250,001	-	$500,000	❑
$500,001	-	$1,000,000	❑
$1,000,001	-	$5,000,000	❑
$5,000,001	+		❑

Other

____

____

____

Family Liabilities

Short Term

Credit Cards, Notes

____

Long Term

Home

____

Business

____

Questions

Maturity dates we need to be aware of?

____

Which accounts are you unhappy with?

____

What else would you like to tell us about?

____

____

____

____

____

Family Income Statement

Income

Earned Income ______________________

Investment Income ______________________

Social Security ______________________

Other ______________________

Total ______________________

Expenses

Fixed ______________________

Variable ______________________

Total ______________________

Personal Goals Statement

Which items would you like help with?

____ Increase my standards of living

____ Financial security at retirement

____ Increase my net worth by __________%

____ Reduce my tax burden

____ Pay for college education for my children

____ Provide for my family in the event of my (or my spouse's) death

____ Minimize the cost of probate and estate taxes

____ Control the distribution of assets to my heirs

____ Plan for long-term or nursing home care

____ Buy a house

Other goals:

____

____

____

____

If you could change two things about your current financial situation, what would you change?

1. ____

2. ____

Investment Goals

	Low Priority									High Priority
Return should exceed inflation rate	1	2	3	4	5	6	7	8	9	10
Principle should be safe	1	2	3	4	5	6	7	8	9	10
Investments should be liquid (immediately accessible)	1	2	3	4	5	6	7	8	9	10
Diversification is important	1	2	3	4	5	6	7	8	9	10
I'd like professional asset management	1	2	3	4	5	6	7	8	9	10
I want to reduce my taxable income	1	2	3	4	5	6	7	8	9	10
I want to build tax-free income	1	2	3	4	5	6	7	8	9	10
I am interested in long-term growth	1	2	3	4	5	6	7	8	9	10
I am interested in short-term profits	1	2	3	4	5	6	7	8	9	10

	Low Risk Tolerance									High Risk Tolerance
Rate your risk tolerance level on a scale of 1 to 10	1	2	3	4	5	6	7	8	9	10

Are there any concerns or questions we haven't addressed today?

____

____

____

____

Example of diversification

In an earthquake, which elevator would you prefer?

The best professionals in the world have coaches like Vince Lombardi. Who's your coach?

We want to be your Vince Lombardi....

Since 1931, do you know how many holes in one there have been in the Masters? 9 holes-in-one achieved...Guess how many have won the Green Jacket? ZERO!

We don't shoot for holes-in-one...**we plan for Green Jackets**!

Notes

5151 Jefferson Blvd., Ste 100
Louisville, KY 40219
Office: (502) 961-6550 • Fax: (502) 961-6389
E-mail: mark.lamkin@lpl.com
www.marktlamkin.com

Mark T. Lamkin, MBA, RFC
President
Wealth Advisor

Mark T. Lamkin, MBA, RFC

- President, Lamkin Wealth Management
- Registered Principal with Linsco/Private Ledger
- #1 Rep for previous brokerage firm for nine consecutive years in the states of Kentucky & Indiana
- Registered Financial Consultant
- Finance degree from University of Louisville (B.S.) - 1991
- MBA from Bellarmine University - 5/2005
- Licenses: FINRA 6, 7, 24, 63 & 65 through Linsco/Private Ledger
- Licensed in Health & Life

Vision

To enhance our clients' lives by providing the blueprint to achieve their goals, live their dreams, and enrich the world through their legacy.

Mission

To enrich our clients' lives by developing their personal blueprint that allows each client to seek true wealth. By providing proactive wealth solution, we anticipate needs before they arise and help our clients stay in conrol of their financial future.

Unique features of our firm

Through Financial Life Planning, we will spend the time to understand you and your unique needs and tailor a plan that will help you reach your goals. Furthermore, as a comprehensive wealth management firm, we offer our clients the following assurances:

- No investment banking relationships
- Access to institutional managers
- Access to no load products
- Investment analysis
- Independent, unbiased advice
- Strategic asset management through Linsco/Private Ledger
- Tax advantage investing
- Estate Planning

Linsco/Private Ledger Highlights

- Nations #1 independent brokerage firm for nine consecutive years. (as reported by Financial Planning Magazine, June 1996-2004)
- 5,000 reps nationwide with $891 million in revenues
- $21 billion in advisory accounts

Providing world class "wealth-care" since 1991

A Future of Fulfillment

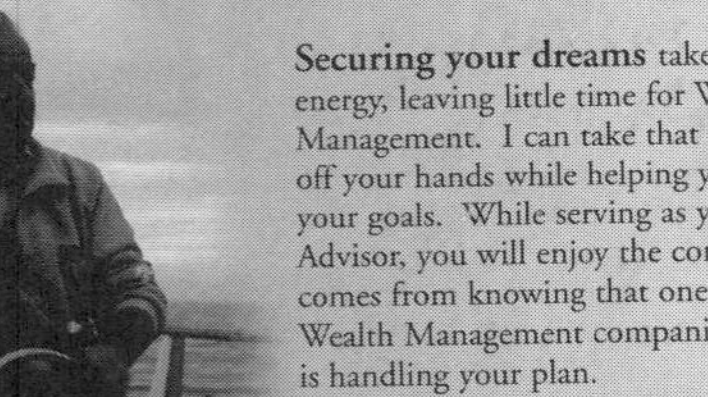

Since 1991, I havebeenproviding financial securityto clientswith my personalizedapproach to wealth planning, accumulationand preservation

Securing your dreams takes effort and energy, leaving little time for Wealth Management. I can take that responsibility off your hands while helping you achieve your goals. While serving as your Wealth Advisor, you will enjoy the confidence that comes from knowing that one of the leading Wealth Management companies in the area is handling your plan.

Since 1991, I have been helping my clients work toward financial security with my personalized approach to wealth planning, accumulation and preservation.

Rest assured that my goal is to help you maintain the standard of living to which you have become accustomed, and to preserve your wealth for your children and grandchildren. In developing and maintaining a well thought-out wealth accumulation plan, we focus on a variety of personalized strategies. We have access to the broadest range of non-proprietary financial products in the industry. We are committed to Independent Products to help accomplish your goals.

At Lamkin Wealth Management, you will work hand-in-hand with Mark Lamkin as your personal wealth advisor to develop your goals. Providing support and expertise to Lamkin Wealth Management is a highly qualified team of financial professionals.

Mark's leadership provides a personal CFO approach that allows our team to get the information they need to help you make the right decisions for your financial future. Regarded as one of the best planners in our area, Mark was his previous companies' top broker for 10 consecutive years. He managed over $100 million dollars and was responsible for ensuring the financial success of each of his clients. Over the last three years, he has put that experience to work at his own Financial Life Planning firm, Lamkin Wealth Management.

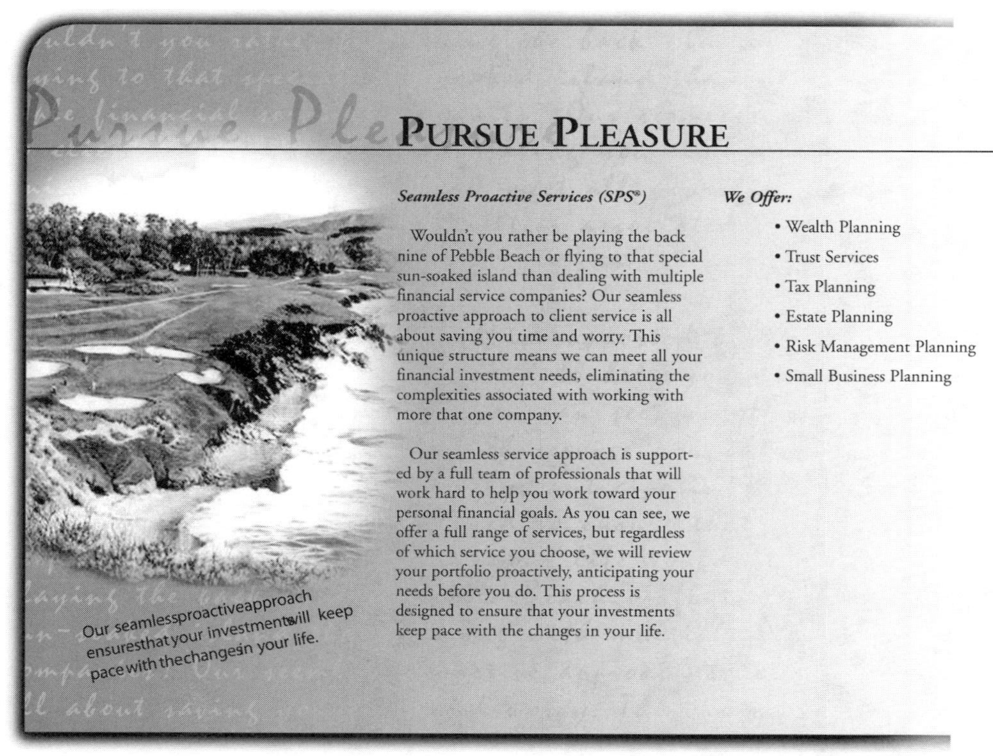
PURSUE PLEASURE
Seamless Proactive Services (SPS®)
Wouldn't you rather be playing the back nine of Pebble Beach or flying to that special sun-soaked island than dealing with multiple financial service companies? Our seamless proactive approach to client service is all about saving you time and worry. This unique structure means we can meet all your financial investment needs, eliminating the complexities associated with working with more that one company.
Our seamless service approach is supported by a full team of professionals that will work hard to help you work toward your personal financial goals. As you can see, we offer a full range of services, but regardless of which service you choose, we will review your portfolio proactively, anticipating your needs before you do. This process is designed to ensure that your investments keep pace with the changes in your life.
We Offer:
• Wealth Planning
• Trust Services
• Tax Planning
• Estate Planning
• Risk Management Planning
• Small Business Planning
Our seamlessproactiveapproach ensuresthatyour investmentswill keep pace with thechangesin your life.

Release Financial Worry to Fully Embrace Life

We can help you maximize theamountof free time you so richly deserve.

There's no time like the present to prepare for those long-awaited days of pursuing your passions, whether it's learning to play golf or nurturing your grandchildren, We can help you maximize the amount of free time you so richly deserve. By working with us now, we can arrange all the details that will affect your financial future, sparing you and/or your loved ones from having to make difficult decisions later.

Wealth Planning

This is where our specialists in tax, asset allocation, investment research and estate distribution develop a comprehensive accumulation and preservation plan that best meets your needs and goals.

Trust Services

We provide access to comprehensive trust services customized to meet your individual needs through a trust company known as The Private Trust Company, N.A., an affiliate of Linsco Private Ledger Corp. From Revocable Trusts, Charitable Reminder Trusts to Irrevocable Life Insurance Trusts, The Private Trust Company provides the following services:

- Administration
- Tax Impacts/Reporting
- Compliance Matters
- Fiduciary Accountability

Wealth Planning

Our tax planning team will prepare your tax return, provide proactive tax planning or work with your existing tax advisor to develop and implement strategies, allowing you to pay less in income taxes.

Your Greatest Gift to Your Children is Your Legacy

Establishingan estateplan can beoneof themosteffectiveways of providingfor your family and leavinga legacyfor thefuture.

Estate Planning

Establishing an estate plan as part of your comprehensive wealth plan can be one of the most effective ways of lowering estate taxes, while providing for your family and leaving a legacy for the future. We offer the following estate planning services:

- Coordinate with your attorney to implement your estate plan from beginning to end
- Retitle assets to reduce or eliminate estate taxes
- Retitle assets to avoid probate
- Bi-annual estate planning reviews

Risk Management

Our risk management team will evaluate your non-financial risks, such as umbrella coverage, long-term care coverage, life coverage and medical coverage to be sure the unexpected does not put a halt on your future retirement.

Small Business Planning

Our business planning professionals will consult with you to evaluate or establish employee retirement plans, executive compensation and business buy-sell/continuity strategies. We will meet with you and/or the key team members of your organization, on a complimentary basis, to explore how we can best meet your needs.

Financial Management Involves More than Money

Our mission involves guiding you to make the right financial decisions for your financial future. You will enjoy and appreciate the numerous benefits of being a member of the Lamkin Wealth Management family. This alliance entitles you access to industry professionals, education workshops, and a variety of client appreciation events.

Come work with Lamkin Wealth Management-where we strive to enhance our clients' quality of life through our values-based financial life planning strategy. Freeing your mind to enjoy the things that are important to you.

Sample events:

- Financial Management Workshops
- Churchill Downs client appreciation day
- Audubon Country Club dinners and golf outings
- Annual Holiday Brunch
- Private client events tailored to your interests

You will enjoy the numerous benefits of being part of the Lamkin Wealth Management family including access to a variety of educational seminars and client appreciation events.

IT'S OUR JOB...
TO HELP MAKE YOUR DREAMS COME TRUE

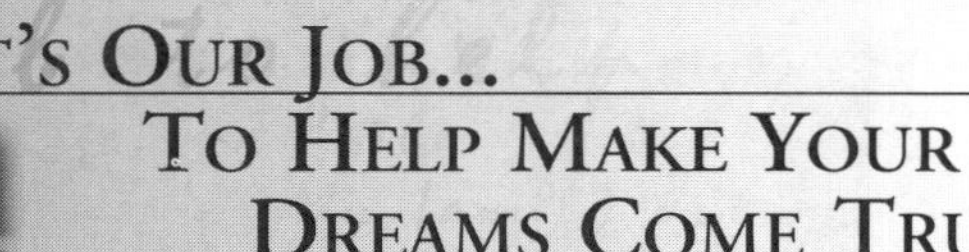

Mark J. Lamkin
Simply the right choice for you and your family.....

LAMKIN WEALTH MANAGEMENT
TAILORED FINANCIAL SERVICES

5151 Jefferson Blvd. Ste 100 • Louisville, KY 40219
Office: (502) 961-6550 • Fax: (502) 961-6389
E-Mail: mark.lamkin@lpl.com
www.lpl.com/mark.lamkin

Securities Offered Through Linsco/Private Ledger Member FINRA/SIPC

My Story....

I grew up in Bullitt County, Kentucky. My family has always been a hard-working, blue collar family. My mother was a bank teller, my father a diesel mechanic. While my mother didn't work until I went to college, my father worked 12-14 hour days to provide for my sister and I. My family knew what it was like to truly live paycheck to paycheck.

While watching my father work hours on end, I decided that I would attend college and learn everything I possibly could about money. After my first finance class, I realized that I had found my passion. As I finished my college degree (Majoring in Finance), I decided my goal would involve educating as many people as I could on the methods of becoming a financial success. Therefore, in 1991, a financial services career was born.

I worked at PNC Brokerage for 10 years. In 2000, I left to build my dream: A successful Financial Life Planning firm. Over the last three years, we have seen tremendous growth in our firm and we hope to serve you as our client.

I tell my story because it's important for you to understand my value system. My father taught me there is no substitute for hard work, determination and honesty. I knew what it was like not to have money and through a successful financial services career, I know what it's like to have money. I like having money better!

As I have aged and as our firm is maturing, I have realized that financial life planning is the best method to help serve clients by integrating financial stewardship with life and financial goals. We hope to work with you many years and develop a partnership that lasts a lifetime.

Personalized Financial Plan

For

John and Mary Sample

March 15, 2005

Prepared by

Silver Financial Planner
P.O. Box 637
Philomath, Oregon 97370

This presentation provides a general overview of some aspects of your personal financial position. It is designed to provide educational and / or general information and is not intended to provide specific legal, accounting, investment, tax or other professional advice. For specific advice on these aspects of your overall financial plan, consult with your professional advisors. Asset or portfolio earnings and / or returns shown, or used in the presentation, are not intended to predict nor guarantee the actual results of any investment products or particular investment style.

IMPORTANT: The illustrations, projections or other information in this report regarding the likelihood of various investment outcomes are hypothetical in nature, and do not reflect actual investment results and are not guarantees of future results. Additionally, it is important to note that information in this report is based upon financial figures input on the date above; results provided may vary with subsequent uses and over time.

Personalized Financial Plan | John and Mary Sample

Information About Your Personalized Financial Plan

We appreciate that you have questions and concerns as you work to attain and preserve financial security. Today's financial environment is complex and in many regards, uncertain. The decisions you make regarding work, spending, investment, and retirement, both now and in the future, will significantly affect your financial condition over the long term.

In an effort to aid you in learning, understanding, and formulating a personal basis for decision making, this 'Personalized Financial Plan' is offered to help enhance your knowledge of various topics and communicate some of the intricacies of the financial world. The plan represents a framework to clarify and structure your financial matters.

This plan is based upon confidential information you provided regarding your present resources and objectives. While illustrations within this plan can be a valuable aid in the examination of your finances, it does not represent the culmination of your planning efforts. Financial planning is an ongoing process.

This hypothetical illustration of mathematical principals is custom made to model some potential situations and transitions you may face in your financial future. Hypothetical assumptions used in this illustration are specifically chosen to communicate and demonstrate your current financial position and highlight for discussion with your advisor the complex future interacting effects of combined incomes, expenses, savings, asset growth, taxes, retirement benefits, and insurance.

This document is not an advertisement or solicitation for any specific investment, investment strategy, or service. No recommendations or projections of specific investments or investment strategies are made or implied. Any illustrations of asset growth contained herein are strictly used to demonstrate mathematical concepts and relationships while presenting a balanced and complete picture of certain financial principles. Growth assumptions are applied to generalized accounts based upon differing tax treatment. Illustrations, charts and tables do not predict or project actual future investment performance, or imply that any past performance will recur.

This plan does not provide tax or legal advice, but may illustrate some tax rules or effects and mention potential legal options for educational purposes. Information contained herein is not a substitute for consultation with a competent legal professional or tax advisor and should only be used in conjunction with his or her advice.

The results shown in this illustration are not guarantees of, or projections of future performance. Results shown are for illustrative purposes only. This presentation contains forward-looking statements and there can be no guarantees that the views and opinions expressed will come to to pass. Historical data shown represents past performance and does not imply or guarantee comparable future results. Information and statistical data contained herein have been obtained from sources believed to be reliable but in no way are guaranteed as to accuracy or completeness.

On page 3, Assumptions, is information provided by you and used throughout the presentation. Please review the information for accuracy and notify your Financial Advisor promptly if discrepancies in the assumptions are present; discrepancies may materially alter the presentation.

Your actual future investment returns, tax levels and inflation are unknown. This illustration uses representative assumptions in a financial planning calculation model to generate a report for education and discussion purposes. Do not rely upon the results of this report to predict actual future investment performance, market conditions, tax effects or inflation rates.

Summary

This report uses financial models to present a picture of your current financial situation and illustrations of possible directions your finances may take. Future economic and market conditions are unknown, and will change. The assumptions used are representative of economic and market conditions that could occur, and are designed to promote a discussion of appropriate actions that may need to be taken, now or in the future, to help you manage and maintain your financial situation under changeable conditions.

Your Current Situation:

- You have assets of approximately $433,000
- You have liabilities of approximately $140,000
- Your net worth is approximately $293,000
- You now have $183,000 in working assets and are adding $16,000 per year.

Your Goals:

- John wants to retire at age 62 and Mary wants to retire at age 60.
- Monthly after-tax income needed at that time is $5,000 (in today's dollars).
- You will need the income until the last life expectancy of age 89.
- To meet your education goals you need to save $11,962 annually ($997 monthly).

Planning Details:

- Asset Allocation: Type of Investor - Somewhat Aggressive
- Long-term care assets at risk - $781,738
- Net Estimated Life Insurance Needs Shortage for John: $462,000
- Net Estimated Life Insurance Needs Shortage for Mary: $181,000
- John and Mary do not have wills.
- John and Mary do not have Durable General Powers of Attorney.
- John and Mary do not have Living Wills.
- John and Mary do not have Healthcare Powers of Attorney.

Retirement Analysis

Using the information you provided, calculations have been made to estimate whether your current retirement program will meet your stated retirement goals. The analysis begins now and extends through life expectancy. It includes tax advantaged, taxable investments, defined benefit pensions, if applicable, and Social Security benefits. The analysis calculates growth and depletion of capital assets over time. This analysis is the basis for the following summarized statement.

Actions:

It appears you may run out of money before the last life expectancy age of 89. The range of possible options you might consider to improve your situation include the following:

- Increase the rate of return on your investments.
- Increase your annual savings by $3,200/year ($267/month).
- Reduce your retirement spending needs by $3,300 to $56,700/year ($4,725/month).
- Defer your retirement by about 1 year.
- Combine any of the above and lower the requirements for each.

This report is for informational and educational purposes only. The information and assumptions used are estimates. The resulting calculations are designed to help illustrate financial concepts and general trends.

Assumptions

Client Information:		3/15/05
Names : John and Mary Sample		
First Name 1	John	
First Name 2	Mary	
Birthdate / Age 1		48
Birthdate / Age 2		46
Retirement Age 1		62
Retirement Age 2		60
Life Expectancy 1		85
Life Expectancy 2		89
Alternate life exp. 1		
Alternate life exp. 2		
Risk Tolerance level	Somewhat Aggressive	
Life Insurance 1		
Life Insurance 2		
Term Insurance 1		$300,000
Term Insurance 2		$100,000
Insurance cash value 1		
Insurance cash value 2		
Pension & Social Security Data (Annual):		
Pension-Indv. 1		$0
Pension start age		0
Pension rate (pre ret.)		0.00%
Pension rate (ret.)		0.00%
Pension survivor %		0%
Pension-Indv. 2		$7,200
Pension start age		60
Pension rate (pre ret.)		0.00%
Pension rate (ret.)		2.00%
Pension survivor %		50%
Soc Sec 1 Start age		62
Soc Sec 1 Rate		2.00%
Earned income 1		$90,000
Soc Sec 1 Amt. (if known)		
Soc Sec 2 Start age		62
Soc Sec 2 Rate		2.00%
Earned income 2		$30,000
Soc Sec 2 Amt. (if known)		

Estimated Education Costs	
Total cost at 6% inf.	$176,820

Expenses & Inflation (Annual After-tax):	
Expenses, (pre ret.)	$70,000
Expenses, Survivor (pre ret.)	$60,000
Expenses at Retirement	$60,000
Expenses, Survivor (ret.)	$50,000
Inflation, (pre ret.)	3.00%
Inflation, Survivor(pre ret.)	3.00%
Inflation at Retirement	3.00%
Inflation, Survivor (ret.)	3.00%

Asset Allocation:	Current	Suggested
Cash & Reserves	13.10%	5.00%
Income	24.00%	0.00%
Income & Growth	62.80%	15.00%
Growth	0.00%	40.00%
Aggressive Growth	0.00%	40.00%
Other	0.00%	0.00%
Rate Assumptions (Before & After Retirement):		
Taxable Returns	9.00%	8.00%
Tax-Deferred & Roth Returns	9.00%	8.00%
Tax-Free Returns	5.00%	5.00%
Return on Annuities	7.00%	7.00%
Effective Tax Rates	25.00%	20.00%
Cost Basis for Taxable Assets		100.00%
Cost Basis for Annuity Assets		100.00%
Additions Increase Rate: Taxable		3.00%
Additions Increase Rate: Tax-Def 1		3.00%
Additions Increase Rate: Tax-Def 2		3.00%

Other Incomes After-tax :

Item Description	Start Year	Inc. Rate	Number of years	Amount per year

Other Expenses After-tax :

European vacation	2014	3.00%	1	($20,000)

Note: These assumptions are based upon information provided by you, combined with representative forward looking values intended to provide a reasonable financial plan illustration for education and discussion purposes. The investment returns, tax rates, benefit increase rates, inflation rates, and future expense values used in this report were selected based on your age, assets, income, goals and other information you provided. These assumptions do not presuppose or analyze any particular investments or investment strategy, or represent a guarantee of future results.

Net Worth Statement

John and Mary Sample

March 15, 2005

ASSETS		
Savings and Investments		
Money Market Accounts/Funds	$20,000	
Annuities	30,000	
Municipal Bonds and Funds	10,000	
Stock Mutual Funds	5,000	
		$65,000
Retirement Accounts		
Qualified Plans-John	$100,000	
IRA Assets-Mary	14,000	
Roth IRA Assets-John	2,000	
Roth IRA Assets-Mary	2,000	
		$118,000
Other Assets		
Residence	$200,000	
Personal property	20,000	
Auto	30,000	
		$250,000
TOTAL ASSETS		$433,000
LIABILITIES		
Residence mortgage	$120,000	
Auto Loans	15,000	
Credit Cards	5,000	
		$140,000
NET WORTH (Assets less Liabilities)		$293,000

Note: Potential taxes due on unrealized gains or assets in tax-deferred retirement plans are not accounted for in this Net Worth Statement.

This report, and its hypothetical illustrations, are intended to form a basis for further discussion with your legal, accounting, and financial advisors. Actual future investment returns, taxes and inflation are unknown. Do not rely upon this report to predict future investment performance.

Asset Worksheet

Description	Current Amount	Annual Additions*	Addition Period	Asset Class	Account Taxation	Asset Type
Cash	20,000			Cash/Res.	Taxable (J)	Money market
Municipal Bond Fund	10,000			Income	Tax-Free Asset (J)	Muni bonds & funds
Stock Mutual Funds	5,000	3,000	2005-2018	Inc/Growth	Taxable (J)	Mutual funds (stock)
IRA	14,000			Income	IRA (2)	Stocks
401k	20,000	1,000	2005-2018	Income	Tax-Deferred (1)	Bond mutual funds
401k	80,000	8,000	2005-2018	Inc/Growth	Tax-Deferred (1)	Mutual funds (stock)
Annuity	30,000			Inc/Growth	Annuity (1)	Annuities
Roth IRA	2,000	2,000	2005-2018	Cash/Res.	Roth IRA (1)	Money market
Roth IRA	2,000	2,000	2005-2018	Cash/Res.	Roth IRA (2)	Money market
Totals:	$183,000	$16,000				

*Annual IRA addition amounts used in the analysis are limited to the maximums allowed by law.

Asset Allocation

Developing An Asset Allocation

Asset allocation refers to maintaining your investments in strategic asset classes, such as Cash, Fixed Income, and Equities, in an advantageous manner over time to ensure adequate diversification. It is important to the success of your planning that your asset allocation be consistent with your goals.

Here is a summary of your current asset allocation.

Personal Investments	Current Balances	Cash & Equivalents	Income Assets	Growth Assets	Other Assets*
Money Market Accounts	$20,000	$20,000			
Annuities	30,000			30,000	
Municipal Bonds & Funds	10,000		10,000		
Stock Mutual Funds	5,000			5,000	
	$65,000	$20,000	$10,000	$35,000	
Retirement Plans					
Qualified Plans-John	$100,000		$20,000	$80,000	
IRA Assets-Mary	14,000		14,000		
Roth IRA Assets-John	2,000	2,000			
Roth IRA Assets-Mary	2,000	2,000			
	$118,000	$4,000	$34,000	$80,000	
Total Investment Assets	$183,000	$24,000	$44,000	$115,000	
		13%	24%	63%	
		Current Asset Allocation			

* Other assets are not included in the Current Asset Allocation.

Your Current Asset Allocation

The information from the previous page was used to create the following chart.
It is important to the success of your planning that your asset allocation is consistent with your goals. You should compare your current allocation to the Suggested Asset Allocation below which may be more appropriate and beneficial to your situation.

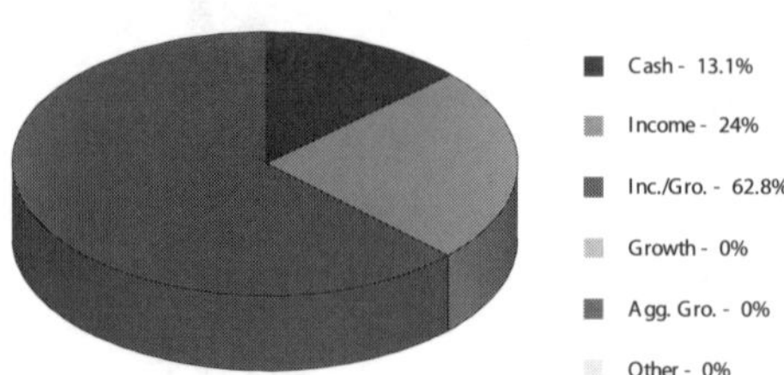

Suggested Asset Allocation (Growth)

Based upon the information you provided, we believe you should consider a growth-oriented investment mix. This allocation has averaged an approximate 10% historical annual return. We have illustrated a broad-based allocation. Effectiveness could be further increased by a blend of large, small, and international stocks within the Equities category. See your Financial Advisor for further analysis.

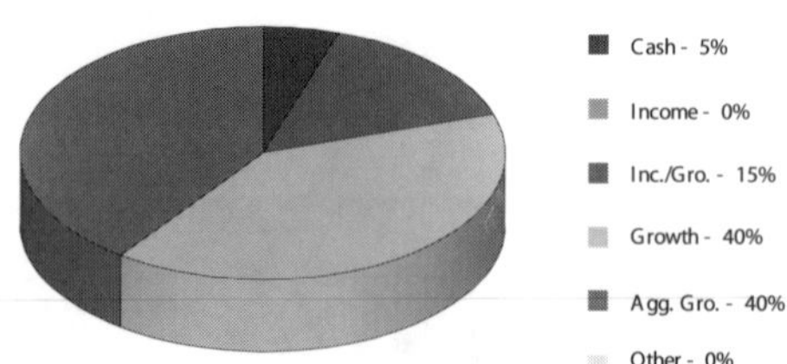

Asset Allocation

	Current		Suggested *			Change
Cash & Reserves	$24,000	13%	$9,150	**	5%	($14,850)
Income	44,000	24%	0		0%	(44,000)
Income & Growth	115,000	63%	27,450		15%	(87,550)
Growth	0	0%	73,200		40%	73,200
Aggressive Growth	0	0%	73,200		40%	73,200
Other	0	0%	0		0%	0
Total	$183,000	100%	$183,000		100%	$0

* These suggested asset allocation percentages are representative portfolio target values.
** Does not include any provision for an Emergency Fund.
Note: Asset Allocation does not guarantee a profit or protect against loss in declining markets.

Retirement Profile

Developing A Retirement Plan

Developing a retirement plan means understanding your current situation, deciding among alternatives, and taking appropriate action today. This report will help you define your current retirement goals, identify your current planning, and estimate the results for your review.

Your Current Retirement Goals

	John	Mary
Age:	48	46
Retirement Age:	62	60
Years until Retirement:	14	14
Years of Retirement:	23	29
Annual Retirement Spending (After-tax):	$60,000	(expressed in today's dollars)

Additional Objectives Please see the attached Education Funding Illustration.

Other Expenses:

European vacation : ($20,000)/year starting 2014, increase rate of 3.00%, for 1 year.

Assumptions

	Pre-Retirement	Retirement
Inflation Rate:	3.0%	3.0%
Income Tax Rate (Average):	25.0%	20.0%
Return on Investments (Average):	8.5%	7.7%

Current residence(s) will be maintained. Related debt will be paid per existing mortgage(s).

Resources Available for Retirement

Funds to meet your goals can come from several sources: Personal Investments, Retirement Plans, Defined Benefit Pensions, Social Security, and Other Income.

Here is a summary of your situation.

Personal Investments	Current Balances
Money Market Accounts	$20,000
Annuities	30,000
Municipal Bonds & Funds	10,000
Stock Mutual Funds	5,000
	$65,000
Retirement Plans	
Qualified Plans-John	$100,000
IRA Assets-Mary	14,000
Roth IRA Assets-John	2,000
Roth IRA Assets-Mary	2,000
	$118,000
Total Investment Assets	$183,000

* See Asset Worksheet for detailed annual savings information.

Social Security	John	Mary
Starting Age	62	62
Benefit at Starting Age (After-tax)	$18,578	$11,210

Pension Plans	John	Mary
Pension Amount per Year (After-tax)	N/A	$5,760
Pension Starting Age		60
Increase Rate Pre-Retirement		0.0%
Increase Rate in Retirement		2.0%
Survivor Percentage		50%

Retirement Summary

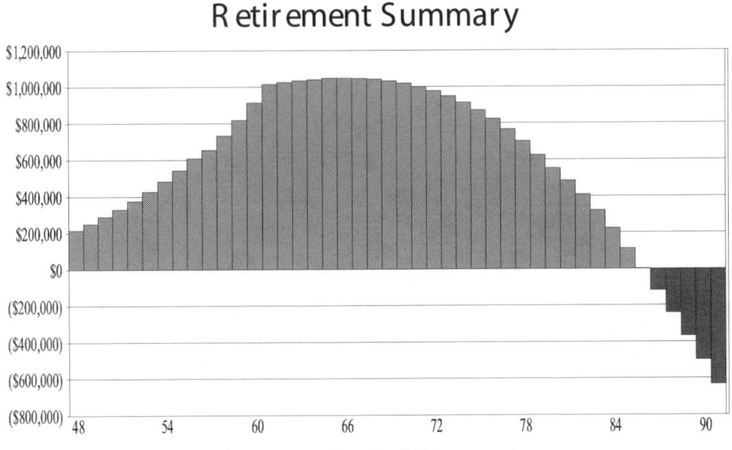

Retirement Capital Illustration

The analysis begins at your current age and extends through your life expectancy. It includes all assets, both tax advantaged and taxable, all expenses, including education funding if applicable, other income and expense estimates, defined benefit pensions, and Social Security benefits. The graph illustrates the growth and depletion of your capital assets, and in cases of capital shortages shows accumulating deficits.

General Assumptions:

Rates of Return Before and After Retirement Used in Illustration:		
Taxable RORs:	9%	8%
Tax Def. RORs:	9%	8%
Tax Free RORs:	5%	5%
Annuity RORs:	7%	7%

Retirement Spending Needs*	$60,000
Survivor Spending Needs*	$50,000
Retirement Age	John - 62
Retirement Age	Mary - 60
Inflation - Current	3%
Inflation - Retirement	3%
Tax Rate - Current	25%
Tax Rate - Retirement	20%

* Spending needs are stated in today's after tax-dollars. See Assumptions page for complete listing of assumptions.

Actual future returns, taxes, expenses, and benefits are unknown. This illustration uses representative estimates and assumptions for educational and discussion purposes only. Do not rely on this report for investment analysis.

Retirement Capital Illustration Results:

It appears you may run out of money before the last life expectancy age of 89.

There are several steps you might consider to improve your situation:

- Increase the rate of return on your investments.
- Add $3,200 more money each year to your savings and investments.
- Reduce the amount you plan to spend in your retirement by $3,300.
- Defer your retirement by about 1 years.

Retirement Expense Forecast

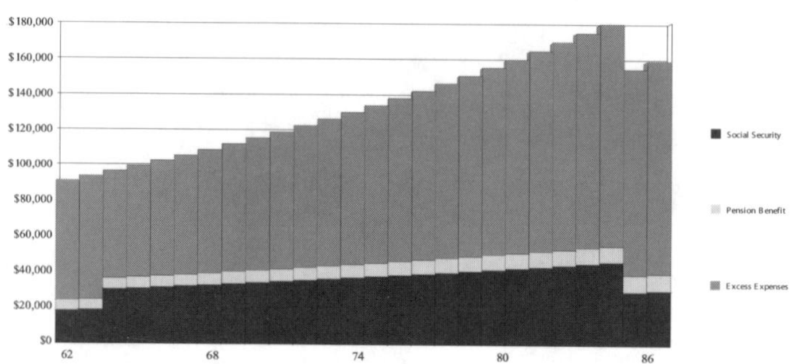

The Retirement Expense Forecast graph combines estimated Social Security benefits with defined pension benefits plotted with estimated annual living expenses in retirement. The graph begins at retirement age and continues to life expectancy. Future retirement expenses are estimated based on your objectives, adjusted for inflation over time. Survivor expense levels start the year after first life expectancy.

Social Security benefits, and annual adjustments for benefit growth, are estimated and illustrated over the anticipated lifetime. If the starting age selected for Social Security benefits is prior to normal benefit age, only a partial Social Security benefit may be available. Benefit amounts may decrease upon first death.

The Pension Benefit estimate combines any pension benefits and plots them starting at the age the benefit begins. At the death of the pension holder a surviving spouse might receive no continuing benefit, or only a portion of the benefit, causing a decrease in overall annual income.

Excess Expenses shown in the graph represent the amount of inflation adjusted annual living expenses that exceed the combined estimated Social Security and pension benefits. These are estimated amounts which will need to come from retirement savings to fund future expenses not covered by expected benefit income.

Note: Social Security and Pension benefit estimates are based upon information you provided. Estimates are not of future benefits amounts. Clients should not rely upon results of this report to predict actual future benefit amounts.

Cash Flow Summary

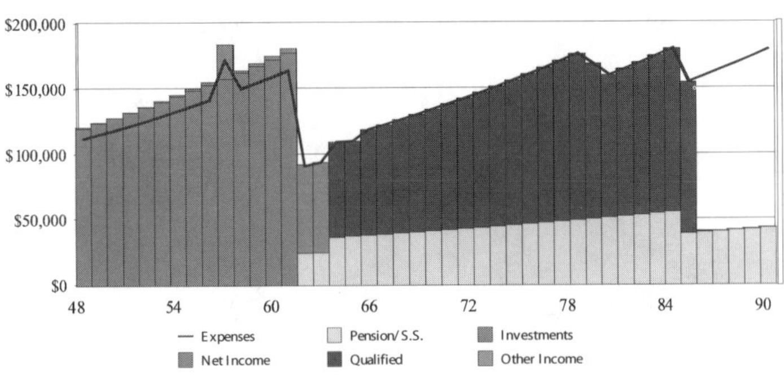

The bars in the above graph represent the amounts available from:

- Earned income (wages and self-employment net of investment)
- Social security
- Qualified plan additions and distributions
- Investment additions and distributions
- Misc - (inheritances, sale of residence, retirement account minimum distributions, life insurance)

The line illustrates the annual expenses including:

- Personal living expenses
- Planned debt expenses
- Specified special expenses and education expenses
- Planned deposits to investment and retirement accounts
- Miscellaneous expense items
- Taxes

Note: The Cash Flow report provides the actual numbers that create the preceding Cash Flow Summary graph.

Cash Flow

Ages Indv. 1	Ages Indv. 2	Earned Income	Retire/Roth Accounts*	Investment Accounts*	Pension/ Soc. Sec.	Other Income	Total Sources	Less Living Expense & Taxes	Shortage or Surplus
		Cash Flow Sources							
48	46	$120,000	($13,000)	($711)			$106,288	($97,750)	$8,538
49	47	123,600	(13,390)	(450)			109,759	(100,682)	9,077
50	48	127,308	(13,790)	(162)			113,355	(103,702)	9,653
51	49	131,126	(14,204)	155			117,076	(106,814)	10,262
52	50	135,060	(14,631)	503			120,931	(110,018)	10,913
53	51	139,112	(15,069)	884			124,926	(113,319)	11,607
54	52	143,285	(15,522)	1,301			129,063	(116,718)	12,345
55	53	147,584	(15,986)	1,757			133,354	(120,220)	13,134
56	54	152,012	(16,466)	2,254			137,799	(123,826)	13,973
57	55	156,572	(16,960)	21,272		(26,095)	134,788	(127,541)	7,247
58	56	161,269	(17,469)	1,565			145,365	(131,367)	13,998
59	57	166,108	(17,994)	2,084			150,197	(135,308)	14,889
60	58	171,090	(18,533)	2,650			155,206	(139,368)	15,838
61	59	176,224	(19,090)	3,266			160,400	(143,549)	16,851
62	60			67,409	24,338		91,746	(90,756)	990
63	61			68,655	24,824		93,479	(93,479)	
64	62		71,027	1,184	36,528		108,738	(108,738)	
65	63		72,083		37,254		109,337	(109,337)	
66	64		80,180		38,002		118,182	(118,182)	
67	65		83,059		38,762		121,821	(121,821)	
68	66		86,038		39,535		125,573	(125,573)	
69	67		89,107		40,331		129,438	(129,438)	
70	68		92,295		41,130		133,425	(133,425)	
71	69		95,566		41,962		137,528	(137,528)	
72	70		98,961		42,798		141,759	(141,759)	
73	71		102,461		43,657		146,118	(146,118)	
74	72		106,091		44,521		150,612	(150,613)	
75	73		109,821		45,420		155,241	(155,241)	
76	74		113,690		46,323		160,013	(160,013)	
77	75		117,677		47,251		164,928	(164,928)	
78	76		121,800		48,195		169,995	(169,995)	
79	77		126,050		49,164		175,214	(175,214)	
80	78		117,530		50,140		167,670	(167,670)	
81	79		107,988		51,151		159,139	(159,139)	
82	80		111,743		52,169		163,912	(163,913)	
83	81		115,615		53,214		168,829	(168,830)	
84	82		119,618		54,277		173,895	(173,895)	
85	83		123,745		55,367		179,112	(179,112)	
	84		114,593		39,145		153,738	(153,738)	
	85		780		39,925		40,705	(158,350)	(117,645)
	86				40,726		40,726	(163,101)	(122,375)
	87				41,540		41,540	(167,994)	(126,454)
	88				42,366		42,366	(173,034)	(130,668)
	89				43,215		43,215	(178,225)	(135,010)

* Scheduled distributions, interest, or dividends taken in cash or amounts taken to meet the IRS minimum distribution requirements.
Note: Earned Income is reduced by qualified retirement account contributions in calculating the effect of income taxes. Pension, Social Security, and Other Income cash flow items are net of income taxes. The tax rate used is the average tax rate entered in the input.

Cash Flow Explanation

Cash flows are sources and uses of money. Primary sources of funds are income from work, Social Security, pensions, savings, insurance proceeds, and other income events. Regular living expenses, education costs, and other planned expenses are the primary use of funds.

The cash flow report pages are designed to be an alternate presentation of the financial information shown elsewhere in this report. The emphasis of the cash flow illustrations are the amounts and types of incomes and levels of expenses that occur during the illustration.

The Cash Flow Summary Graph illustrates four primary financial elements; income, investment, expenses, and cash sources. The different colored bars in the graph represent the level of cash flows that are occurring, and what accounts they are related to. The single solid line represents the annual expense level from now to the end of the illustration. Prior to retirement, bars above the expense level represent investments.

Portions of bars below the expense line represent sources of cash that are being used to pay for planned living expenses and to cover special expenses such as education. During the working years, income from employment is generally the primary source of cash to cover expenses. In retirement, social security, pension benefits, and cash withdrawn from investment accounts are the major sources of cash to cover expenses.

In general terms, the best case is to have the cash flow bars always at or above the expense line. This indicates that there is sufficient income, or investment asset sources, to meet living expenses and other planned needs. Gaps between the expense line and cash flow bars indicate calculated shortfalls of cash flow during those years.

The cash flow numbers page contains the numerical information upon which the graph is based. This page shows the sources and uses of funds. The columns coincide with the bars and lines in the cash flow graph. Red numbers represent a use of cash, black a source.

The red numbers in the RetireR oth or Investment ccounts columns are additions made to those accounts; these are investments and uses of funds. The black numbers in those columns represent withdrawals from the account; these are sources of funds to meet retirement needs.

ll sources and investment uses are subtotaled in the Total Sources column. Tax estimates are based on earned income and investment income adjusted for contributions to u alified retirement accounts multiplied by the estimated net effective tax rates. The resulting tax estimate is added to inflation adjusted living expenses to create an estimated annual figure.

The combination of Total Sources and i ving x penses Taxes can create a surplus or shortage. shortage indicates that expenses exceed incomes and sources. surplus can indicate that incomes exceed expenses. During retirement, if money is withdrawn at the same level of need, no surplus or shortage will occur.

Total Capital Assets

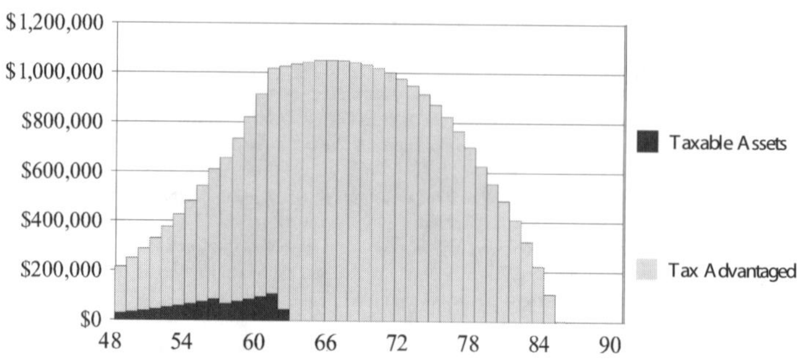

The Total Capital Assets graph displays taxable assets, combined with the value of the tax advantaged assets over time. The illustration shows assets from current age through life expectancy. Estimated capital growth is based on the rate of return for the assets, plus any annual additions or expenses. When the taxable accounts have been consumed, tax-advantaged accounts may be drawn on for additional funds.

Generally, the IRS requires that by age 70 1/2, minimum distributions must be made from qualified tax-deferred accounts. These annual distributions must be made on a schedule calculated to consume the account balances during the life expectancy. Money distributed from these tax-deferred accounts will first be used to meet current spending needs. Excess funds will be reinvested into taxable accounts.

Retirement Capital Analysis

Ages*		Retirement Spending Needs	Sources of Annual Income**				Education & Other Inc/Exp	Net Surplus or (Shortage)	Annual Additions To Assets	Retirement Capital
			Social Security		Pension Income					
			Indv. 1	Indv. 2	Indv. 1	Indv. 2				$183,000
48	46								16,000	214,593
49	47								16,480	249,359
50	48								16,973	287,585
51	49								17,483	329,585
52	50								18,008	375,701
53	51								18,547	426,301
54	52								19,105	481,788
55	53								19,676	542,601
56	54								20,267	609,218
57	55						(26,095)	(26,095)	20,875	655,183
58	56								21,501	733,189
59	57								22,147	818,576
60	58								22,811	912,003
61	59								23,496	1,014,192
62 R	60 R	90,756	18,578			5,760		(66,418)		1,023,675
63	61	93,479	18,949			5,875		(68,655)		1,032,652
64	62	96,283	19,328	11,210		5,990		(59,755)		1,039,616
65	63	99,171	19,715	11,434		6,106		(61,917)		1,047,714
66	64	102,146	20,109	11,663		6,230		(64,144)		1,048,143
67	65	105,210	20,511	11,896		6,355		(66,448)		1,045,609
68	66	108,366	20,921	12,134		6,480		(68,831)		1,039,775
69	67	111,617	21,340	12,376		6,614		(71,286)		1,030,283
70	68	114,966	21,767	12,624		6,739		(73,836)		1,016,717
71	69	118,415	22,202	12,877		6,883		(76,453)		998,662
72	70	121,967	22,646	13,134		7,018		(79,169)		975,633
73	71	125,626	23,099	13,397		7,162		(81,969)		947,122
74	72	129,395	23,561	13,665		7,296		(84,874)		912,553
75	73	133,277	24,032	13,938		7,450		(87,857)		871,341
76	74	137,275	24,513	14,217		7,594		(90,952)		822,808
77	75	141,393	25,003	14,501		7,747		(94,142)		766,245
78	76	145,635	25,503	14,791		7,901		(97,440)		700,870
79	77	150,004	26,013	15,087		8,064		(100,840)		625,846
80	78	154,504	26,533	15,389		8,218		(104,364)		553,681
81	79	159,139	27,064	15,696		8,390		(107,988)		485,666
82	80	163,913	27,605	16,010		8,554		(111,744)		408,305
83	81	168,830	28,157	16,331		8,726		(115,616)		320,728
84	82	173,895	28,721	16,657		8,899		(119,618)		221,983
85	83	179,112	29,295	16,990		9,082		(123,745)		111,046
	84	153,738		29,881		9,264		(114,593)		752
	85	158,350		30,478		9,446		(118,425)		
	86	163,101		31,088		9,638		(122,375)		
	87	167,994		31,710		9,830		(126,454)		
	88	173,034		32,344		10,022		(130,668)		
	89	178,225		32,991		10,224		(135,010)		

*R=Retirement age, L=Life expectancy.** Pensions & 85% of S.S. reduced 20% for income taxes.

Note: Report is based upon assumed inflation rates of 3% and 3% (before and after retirement). Actual future inflation rates are unknown.

Taxable Savings & Investment Accounts

Ages		Account Additions	Annual Growth	Income Tax On Account*	From Tax-Advantaged Assets Distri-butions	Income Tax	Paid out or received for cash flow	Account Balance**
								$25,000
48	46	3,000	2,384	(597)				29,788
49	47	3,090	2,819	(705)				34,992
50	48	3,182	3,292	(824)				40,644
51	49	3,278	3,805	(952)				46,776
52	50	3,376	4,361	(1,091)				53,423
53	51	3,477	4,964	(1,242)				60,624
54	52	3,582	5,617	(1,405)				68,419
55	53	3,689	6,323	(1,581)				76,851
56	54	3,800	7,087	(1,772)				85,967
57	55	3,914	6,738	(1,685)			(26,096)	68,840
58	56	4,031	6,377	(1,595)				77,654
59	57	4,152	7,175	(1,794)				87,188
60	58	4,277	8,039	(2,010)				97,494
61	59	4,405	8,972	(2,244)				108,629
62R	60R		6,033	(1,207)			(66,419)	47,037
63	61		1,823	(365)	20,159		(68,655)	
64	62				72,210	(12,456)	(59,755)	
65	63				72,083	(10,167)	(61,917)	
66	64				80,180	(16,037)	(64,145)	
67	65				83,059	(16,612)	(66,448)	
68	66				86,038	(17,208)	(68,831)	
69	67				89,107	(17,822)	(71,287)	
70	68				92,295	(18,460)	(73,837)	
71	69				95,566	(19,114)	(76,454)	
72	70				98,961	(19,793)	(79,170)	
73	71				102,461	(20,493)	(81,969)	
74	72				106,091	(21,219)	(84,874)	
75	73				109,821	(21,965)	(87,858)	
76	74				113,690	(22,739)	(90,953)	
77	75				117,677	(23,536)	(94,142)	
78	76				121,800	(24,361)	(97,441)	
79	77				126,050	(25,211)	(100,841)	
80	78				117,530	(13,167)	(104,365)	
81	79				107,988		(107,989)	
82	80				111,743		(111,744)	
83	81				115,615		(115,616)	
84	82				119,618		(119,619)	
85L	83				123,745		(123,746)	
	84				114,593		(114,594)	
	85				780		(118,426)	
	86						(122,375)	
	87						(126,454)	
	88						(130,668)	
	89L						(135,011)	

* Estimated taxes include tax due on income and on sales of assets. Starting cost basis is estimated at 100%.

** This report is based on assumed growth rates of 9.00% and 8.00%, and inflation rates of 3.00% and 3.00% (before and after retirement). Account additions are calculated to increase at 3.00% per year for each individual.

Tax-Deferred Annuities

Ages 1 & 2	Account Additions	Annual Growth	Account Withdrawals	Balance* $30,000	Cumulative Growth	Taxable Withdrawal	Income Tax Due
48 46		2,100		32,100	2,100		
49 47		2,247		34,347	4,347		
50 48		2,404		36,751	6,751		
51 49		2,573		39,324	9,324		
52 50		2,753		42,077	12,077		
53 51		2,945		45,022	15,022		
54 52		3,152		48,173	18,173		
55 53		3,372		51,546	21,546		
56 54		3,608		55,154	25,154		
57 55		3,861		59,015	29,015		
58 56		4,131		63,146	33,146		
59 57		4,420		67,566	37,566		
60 58		4,730		72,295	42,295		
61 59		5,061		77,356	47,356		
62R 60R		5,415		82,771	52,771		
63 61		5,794		88,565	58,565		
64 62		3,714	(71,027)	21,251	62,278	62,278	(12,456)
65 63		719	(21,970)		719	719	(144)
66 64							
67 65							
68 66							
69 67							
70 68							
71 69							
72 70							
73 71							
74 72							
75 73							
76 74							
77 75							
78 76							
79 77							
80 78							
81 79							
82 80							
83 81							
84 82							
85 83							
86 84							
87 85							
88 86							
89 87							
90 88							
91 89							

* This report is based on assumed growth rates of 7.00% and 7.00%, with inflation rates of 3.00% and 3.00% (before and after retirement). Starting cost basis is 100%. Account additions are calculated to increase 3.00% per year.

Tax-Deferred Retirement Accounts

	Individual 1 Accounts					Individual 2 Accounts			
Age	Account Additions	Annual Growth	With-drawals	Balance* $100,000	Age	Account Additions	Annual Growth	With-drawals	Balance* $14,000
48	9,000	9,405		118,405	46		1,260		15,260
49	9,270	11,073		138,748	47		1,373		16,633
50	9,548	12,916		161,213	48		1,496		18,129
51	9,834	14,951		185,999	49		1,631		19,760
52	10,129	17,195		213,324	50		1,778		21,538
53	10,433	19,668		243,426	51		1,938		23,476
54	10,746	22,391		276,564	52		2,112		25,588
55	11,068	25,388		313,021	53		2,302		27,890
56	11,400	28,684		353,106	54		2,510		30,400
57	11,742	32,307		397,156	55		2,736		33,136
58	12,095	36,288		445,539	56		2,982		36,118
59	12,458	40,659		498,656	57		3,250		39,368
60	12,831	45,456		556,944	58		3,543		42,911
61	13,216	50,719		620,880	59		3,861		46,772
62		49,670		670,550	60		3,741		50,513
63		53,644		724,194	61		4,041		54,554
64		57,935		782,129	62		4,364		58,918
65		60,565	50,114	792,581	63		4,713		63,631
66		60,199	80,181	772,600	64		5,090		68,721
67		58,485	83,060	748,025	65		5,497		74,218
68		56,400	86,039	718,386	66		5,937		80,155
69		53,906	89,108	683,184	67		6,412		86,567
70		50,962	92,296	641,851	68		6,925		93,492
71		47,525	95,567	593,809	69		7,479		100,971
72		43,693	95,277	542,225	70		7,930	3,686	105,216
73		39,438	98,491	483,172	71		8,258	3,971	109,504
74		34,581	101,815	415,938	72		8,589	4,278	113,815
75		29,066	105,214	339,790	73		8,920	4,608	118,127
76		22,834	108,727	253,897	74		9,251	4,964	122,415
77		15,818	112,332	157,383	75		9,579	5,346	126,648
78		7,948	116,044	49,288	76		9,901	5,757	130,792
79		1,895	51,184		77		7,468	74,867	63,394
80					78		2,438	65,833	
81					79				
82					80				
83					81				
84					82				
85					83				
					84				
					85				
					86				
					87				
					88				
					89				

* This report is based on assumed growth rates of 9.00% and 8.00%, with inflation rates of 3.00% and 3.00% (before and after retirement). Account deposits are calculated to increase 3.00% and 3.00% per year (Individual 1 and 2).

Tax-Free Accounts

Combined ROTH IRA Accounts							Other Tax Free Assets			
Age Indv 1	Age Indv 2	Additions Indv. 1	Additions Indv. 2	Annual Growth	With-drawals	Balance* $4,000	Account Additions	Annual Growth	With-drawals	Balance* $10,000
48	46	2,000	2,000	540		8,540		500		10,500
49	47	2,060	2,060	954		13,614		525		11,025
50	48	2,121	2,121	1,416		19,272		551		11,576
51	49	2,185	2,185	1,931		25,572		579		12,154
52	50	2,251	2,251	2,504		32,578		608		12,761
53	51	2,318	2,318	3,141		40,354		638		13,399
54	52	2,388	2,388	3,847		48,976		670		14,068
55	53	2,459	2,459	4,629		58,522		703		14,771
56	54	2,533	2,533	5,495		69,082		739		15,509
57	55	2,609	2,609	6,452		80,752		775		16,284
58	56	2,687	2,687	7,510		93,634		814		17,098
59	57	2,768	2,768	8,676		107,846		855		17,952
60	58	2,851	2,851	9,963		123,510		898		18,849
61	59	2,937	2,937	11,380		140,764		942		19,791
62R	60R			11,261		152,024		990		20,780
63	61			12,162		164,184		535	(20,159)	1,155
64	62			13,135		177,318		28	(1,183)	
65	63			14,185		191,502				
66	64			15,320		206,822				
67	65			16,546		223,366				
68	66			17,869		241,234				
69	67			19,299		260,532				
70	68			20,843		281,374				
71	69			22,510		303,882				
72	70			24,311		328,192				
73	71			26,255		354,446				
74	72			28,356		382,800				
75	73			30,624		413,424				
76	74			33,074		446,496				
77	75			35,720		482,214				
78	76			38,577		520,790				
79	77			41,663		562,452				
80	78			42,928	(51,699)	553,681				
81	79			39,975	(107,988)	485,666				
82	80			34,384	(111,744)	408,305				
83	81			28,040	(115,616)	320,728				
84	82			20,874	(119,618)	221,983				
85	83			12,809	(123,745)	111,046				
	84			4,300	(114,593)	752				
	85			29	(781)					
	86									
	87									
	88									
	89									

* Roth growth rates: 9.00% and 8.00%, Tax-Free: 5.00% and 5.00%, inflation rates: 3.00% and 3.00% (before and after retirement). Account deposits are calculated to increase 3.00% and 3.00% per year (Individual 1 and 2).

Insurance Summary

Company Name	0	0
Insured	Indv. 1	Indv. 2
Owner	Indv. 1	Indv. 2
Beneficiary	Indv. 2	Indv. 1
Type	0	0
Death Benefit	$300,000	$100,000
Annual Premium		
Total Premiums Paid		
Current Cash Values		

Insurance Included in Estate:

John predeceases Mary

	John	Mary
Policy 1 - 0	$300,000	$0
Policy 2 - 0	0	100,000
	$300,000	$100,000

Mary predeceases John

	Mary	John
Policy 1 - 0	$0	$300,000
Policy 2 - 0	100,000	0
	$100,000	$300,000

Survivor Needs Analysis

John and Mary Sample

In the event of an untimely death, survivors may be left without the household income needed to sustain their existing lifestyle. Life insurance coverage is recommended in an amount that will ensure sufficient ongoing income, as well as cover immediate needs, such as final expenses.

Determining proper levels of life insurance involves a comparison of current and future household expense levels with expected surviving spouse's earnings plus survivor benefits. Other resources are also taken into account such as: liquid assets, investments, pension, and retirement accounts.

Insurance needs estimates are the calculated lump sum amounts which would provide a source of future cash flow to supplement the anticipated household income. The insurance levels suggested are just general guides and may not include all factors affecting your own situation.

Spending needs for this report are based upon $60,000 per year, inflated at 3% each year until retirement and $50,000 per year, inflated at 3% each year during retirement.

Life Insurance Basic Needs Estimate on John:

Present Value:	Anticipated Spending Needs	$1,305,768	
	Education Expenses	100,000	
	Other Expenses	32,946	$1,438,714
	Mary's Employment	($248,235)	
	Social Security Benefits	(341,733)	
	Pension Benefits	(43,582)	
	Other Incomes	(0)	($633,550)

Net Estimated Survivor Need Shortage	$805,164
Currently Existing Liabilities	140,000
Assets Available to Offset Shortage	(183,000)
Current Life Insurance Coverage	(300,000)
Suggested Additional Life Insurance Coverage	$462,164

Note: Estimated insurance requirements can vary over time due to changes in asset levels, special expenses, education expenses, estate planning, and spousal retirement needs. Additional insurance, held outside of an insurance trust, may have estate tax consequences. It may be prudent to purchase an amount of insurance appropriate to prepare for potential higher coverage needs. Consult with your financial advisor about factors that may suggest additional insurance coverage.

Survivor Needs Analysis

John and Mary Sample

In the event of an untimely death, survivors may be left without the household income needed to sustain their existing lifestyle. Life insurance coverage is recommended in an amount that will ensure sufficient ongoing income, as well as cover immediate needs, such as final expenses.

Determining proper levels of life insurance involves a comparison of current and future household expense levels with expected surviving spouse's earnings plus survivor benefits. Other resources are also taken into account such as: liquid assets, investments, pension, and retirement accounts.

Insurance needs estimates are the calculated lump sum amounts which would provide a source of future cash flow to supplement the anticipated household income. The insurance levels suggested are just general guides and may not include all factors affecting your own situation.

Spending needs for this report are based upon $60,000 per year, inflated at 3% each year until retirement and $50,000 per year, inflated at 3% each year during retirement.

Life Insurance Basic Needs Estimate on Mary:

Present Value:	Anticipated Spending Needs	$1,217,184	
	Education Expenses	100,000	
	Other Expenses	32,946	$1,350,130
	John's Employment	($744,705)	
	Social Security Benefits	(246,335)	
	Pension Benefits	(34,884)	
	Other Incomes	(0)	($1,025,924)

Net Estimated Survivor Need Shortage	$324,206
Currently Existing Liabilities	140,000
Assets Available to Offset Shortage	(183,000)
Current Life Insurance Coverage	(100,000)
Suggested Additional Life Insurance Coverage	$181,206

Note: Estimated insurance requirements can vary over time due to changes in asset levels, special expenses, education expenses, estate planning, and spousal retirement needs. Additional insurance, held outside of an insurance trust, may have estate tax consequences. It may be prudent to purchase an amount of insurance appropriate to prepare for potential higher coverage needs. Consult with your financial advisor about factors that may suggest additional insurance coverage.

 This report, and its hypothetical illustrations, are intended to form a basis for further discussion with your legal, accounting, and financial advisors. Actual future investment returns, taxes and inflation are unknown. Do not rely upon this report to predict future investment performance.

Survivor Needs Calculation for Mary, To Estimate Life Insurance Required on John

NPV's*	($1,305,768)	($100,000)	($32,946)	$248,235	$341,733	$43,582	($805,164)
Age	After Tax Spending Need	Education Costs	Other Inc/Exp**	After Tax Emp. Income	After Tax SS Benefits	After Tax Pension Inc.	Estimated Inc. Shortage
46	(60,000)		(17,500)	22,500	32,810		(22,190)
47	(61,800)			23,175	33,467		(5,158)
48	(63,654)			23,870	34,136		(5,648)
49	(65,564)			24,586	34,819		(6,159)
50	(67,531)			25,324	30,441		(11,765)
51	(69,556)	(12,624)		26,084	31,050		(25,047)
52	(71,643)	(20,073)		26,866	31,671		(33,179)
53	(73,792)	(21,278)		27,672	32,305		(35,094)
54	(76,006)	(22,554)		28,502			(70,058)
55	(78,286)	(23,908)	(26,095)	29,357			(98,932)
56	(80,635)	(25,342)		30,238			(75,739)
57	(83,054)	(26,863)		31,145			(78,772)
58	(85,546)			32,080			(53,466)
59	(88,112)			33,042			(55,070)
60	(75,629)				16,317	5,760	(53,553)
61	(77,898)				16,643	5,875	(55,380)
62	(80,235)				19,328	5,990	(54,917)
63	(82,642)				19,715	6,106	(56,822)
64	(85,122)				20,109	6,230	(58,782)
65	(87,675)				20,511	6,355	(60,809)
66	(90,306)				20,921	6,480	(62,904)
67	(93,015)				21,340	6,614	(65,061)
68	(95,805)				21,767	6,739	(67,299)
69	(98,679)				22,202	6,883	(69,594)
70	(101,640)				22,646	7,018	(71,976)
71	(104,689)				23,099	7,162	(74,428)
72	(107,830)				23,561	7,296	(76,973)
73	(111,064)				24,032	7,450	(79,583)
74	(114,396)				24,513	7,594	(82,290)
75	(117,828)				25,003	7,747	(85,078)
76	(121,363)				25,503	7,901	(87,959)
77	(125,004)				26,013	8,064	(90,927)
78	(128,754)				26,533	8,218	(94,003)
79	(132,617)				27,064	8,390	(97,162)
80	(136,595)				27,605	8,554	(100,436)
81	(140,693)				28,157	8,726	(103,809)
82	(144,914)				28,721	8,899	(107,294)
83	(149,261)				29,295	9,082	(110,885)
84	(153,739)				29,881	9,264	(114,594)
85	(158,351)				30,478	9,446	(118,427)
86	(163,102)				31,088	9,638	(122,375)
87	(167,995)				31,710	9,830	(126,455)
88	(173,035)				32,344	10,022	(130,668)
89	(178,226)				32,991	10,224	(135,011)

* Net Present Values for this illustration are calculated using an after-tax discount rate of 6% (Education Costs at 6%)

** First year expenses include allowance for final expenses and emergency funds in the amount of $17,500.

Survivor Needs Calculation for John, To Estimate Life Insurance Required on Mary

NPV's*	($1,217,184)	($100,000)	($32,946)	$744,705	$246,335	$34,884	($324,206)
Age	After Tax Spending Need	Education Costs	Other Inc/Exp**	After Tax Emp. Income	After Tax SS Benefits	After Tax Pension Inc.	Estimated Inc. Shortage
48	(60,000)		(17,500)	67,500	19,807	1,763	11,570
49	(61,800)			69,525	20,203	1,798	29,726
50	(63,654)			71,611	20,607	1,834	30,398
51	(65,564)			73,759	21,020	1,871	31,086
52	(67,531)			75,972	18,377	1,908	28,726
53	(69,556)	(12,624)		78,251	18,745	1,946	16,761
54	(71,643)	(20,073)		80,599	19,120	1,985	9,987
55	(73,792)	(21,278)		83,016	19,502	2,025	9,473
56	(76,006)	(22,554)		85,507		2,065	(10,988)
57	(78,286)	(23,908)	(26,095)	88,072		2,107	(38,111)
58	(80,635)	(25,342)		90,714		2,149	(13,114)
59	(83,054)	(26,863)		93,436		2,192	(14,290)
60	(85,546)			96,239		2,235	12,929
61	(88,112)			99,126		2,280	13,294
62	(75,629)				18,578	2,481	(54,571)
63	(77,898)				18,949	2,530	(56,419)
64	(80,235)				19,328	2,581	(58,326)
65	(82,642)				19,715	2,633	(60,295)
66	(85,122)				20,109	2,685	(62,327)
67	(87,675)				20,511	2,739	(64,425)
68	(90,306)				20,921	2,794	(66,590)
69	(93,015)				21,340	2,850	(68,825)
70	(95,805)				21,767	2,907	(71,132)
71	(98,679)				22,202	2,965	(73,513)
72	(101,640)				22,646	3,024	(75,970)
73	(104,689)				23,099	3,085	(78,505)
74	(107,830)				23,561	3,146	(81,122)
75	(111,064)				24,032	3,209	(83,823)
76	(114,396)				24,513	3,273	(86,610)
77	(117,828)				25,003	3,339	(89,486)
78	(121,363)				25,503	3,406	(92,454)
79	(125,004)				26,013	3,474	(95,517)
80	(128,754)				26,533	3,543	(98,678)
81	(132,617)				27,064	3,614	(101,939)
82	(136,595)				27,605	3,686	(105,304)
83	(140,693)				28,157	3,760	(108,776)
84	(144,914)				28,721	3,835	(112,358)
85	(149,261)				29,295	3,912	(116,054)

* Net Present Values for this illustration are calculated using an after-tax discount rate of 6% (Education Costs at 6%)

** First year expenses include allowance for final expenses and emergency funds in the amount of $17,500.

Disability Income Insurance

Disability due to illness or injury can devastate your financial plans. At a time when you are unable to work for a living, household expenses may actually increase while your income decreases. You could be forced to deplete funds that might have been saved for your retirement years.

Generally, the goal of disability income insurance is to replace the after-tax earnings of the insured wage earner and to allow you and your family to maintain your current lifestyle. Based on your current situation, you would need to replace the following income if you were disabled.

John-		Mary-	
Current Income:	$90,000/Yr.	Current Income:	$30,000/Yr.
Replacement Ratio*:	65%	Replacement Ratio*:	65%
Suggested Need:	$59,000/Yr.	Suggested Need:	$20,000/Yr.

* Current underwriting standards allow only a portion of Current Income to be replaced.

In addition, there are many factors which could affect the amount of the Suggested Need noted above. You should review these items before making your final decision. These factors include:

- Investment Income
- Investment Assets
- Retirement Assets
- Spouse's Salary
- Pension Income
- Other Income
- Changes in Living Expenses
- Inflation
- Funds required for retirement/education or other needs
- Length of Time Until Retirement
- Changes in Taxes
- Social Security Disability Benefits
- Employer Disability Benefits

Note: Consult with your financial advisor about factors that may suggest additional insurance coverage.

Long-Term Care

Long-Term Care Defined

Long-term care is sustained medical or custodial care in a hospital, nursing facility, or equivalent care at This care meets the needs of people when, for some reason, they cannot care for themselves. Long-term care insurance provides coverage for costs when the need for care extends beyond a pre-determined period. Benefits start when certain conditions and time frames specified by a long-term care insurance policy are

Generally the needs requirements to obtain insurance benefits fall into two categories:

An inability to perform two or more Activities of Daily Living (or ADLs).	Activities of Daily Living (ADLs) are basic functions of daily independent living and includes: Dressing Toileting Bathing Transferring Eating Continence
Impaired Cognitive Ability	Loss of mental function can result from stroke, dementia or Alzheimer's Disease. Alzheimer's Disease is a disorder that progressively affects one's ability to carry out daily activities.

The Cost of Waiting to Plan

- 40% of all long-term care recipients are under the age of 65.
- Over 45% of seniors who reach age 65 will spend some time in a nursing home.
- Over 70% of seniors who reach age 65 will need some form of home health care in their lifetime.
- One out of every four families provides care to an elderly relative or loved one.
- 25% will stay in a Nursing Facility for more than one full year.
- The average nursing home stay is 2.5 years and the average Alzheimer's stay is 7 years.

Without benefits from long-term care insurance or a comparable plan, the cost of providing these services could devastate your lifetime savings, or a relative's life savings. On average, one year in a nursing home costs in the area of $57,000 and can easily exceed $100,000.

Depending on the care required, most of these expenses are paid for by the patient or their family. Medicare may contribute toward the first 100 days expenses in a skilled care facility. There are no Medicaid benefits available for intermediate-term or custodial care, unless the state finds the patient to be impoverished under local guidelines. Even then, care options would be restricted to care facilities that accept the very limited benefit payments Medicaid offers.

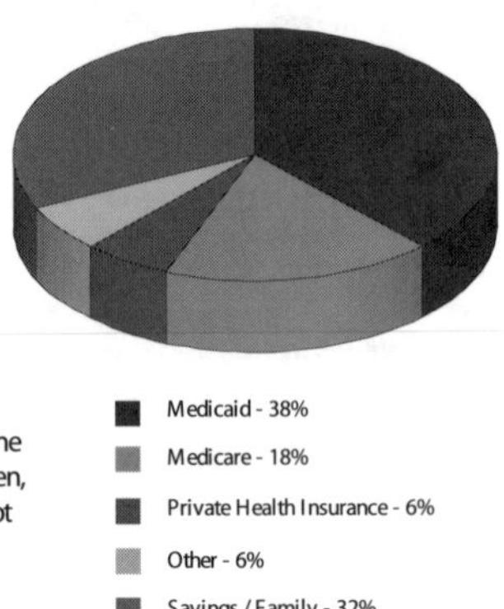

- Medicaid - 38%
- Medicare - 18%
- Private Health Insurance - 6%
- Other - 6%
- Savings / Family - 32%

Medicaid and Medicare Facts

- Medicaid is a welfare program designed as an emergency safety net to pay health care costs of the poor.
- Medicare is part of Social Security, and helps pay for the general health care needs of retired persons.
- Medicare typically only pays for doctors, hospitals, and short recuperative stays in nursing facilities.
- Private health insurance is designed for medical (doctors, hospitals, etc) not long-term care expenses.
- Most people end up relying on their own or relatives resources to pay for long-term care expenses.

Long-Term Care Need Analysis

Long-term care (LTC) requires long-term planning. LTC insurance is available to cover these expenses, protect your assets, your independence, and control the quality of the care you receive. You are able to choose the specified daily benefit level, as well as the types of medical and care services covered.

When is the best time to purchase LTC insurance? Generally, the premiums stay level once the policy is purchased, much like level term insurance. In practice, the earlier you buy a policy, the lower the premium. Since the odds of becoming disabled increase with age, purchasing coverage before the age of 55 is good planning. Consider the premium cost of several coverage levels to determine which is right for your budget.

Needs Estimate

These estimated long-term care cost examples are based upon your financial information. Consider the numbers here to be a starting point for analysis and discussion of your long-term care insurance needs.

	John	Mary
Estimated daily care cost	$200	$200
Estimated annual care costs	$73,000	$73,000
Estimated years of care	5	5
Assumed inflation rate	5%	5%

Current financial assets exposed to potential long-term care expense $183,000

Depending on your age, a delay in arranging a Long-term care policy can mean substantially higher premiums. This graph illustrates the cost of waiting to purchase a Long-term care policy.

A Long-term care policy can stabilize and moderate the potentially damaging costs of nursing home care. This graph displays potential cost differential and value of having a Long-term insurance plan in place.

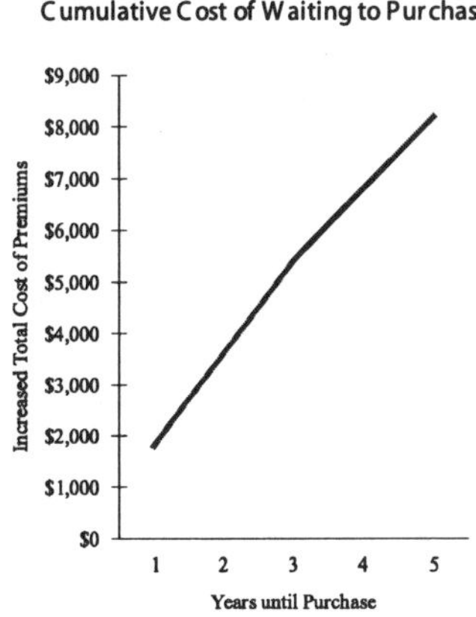

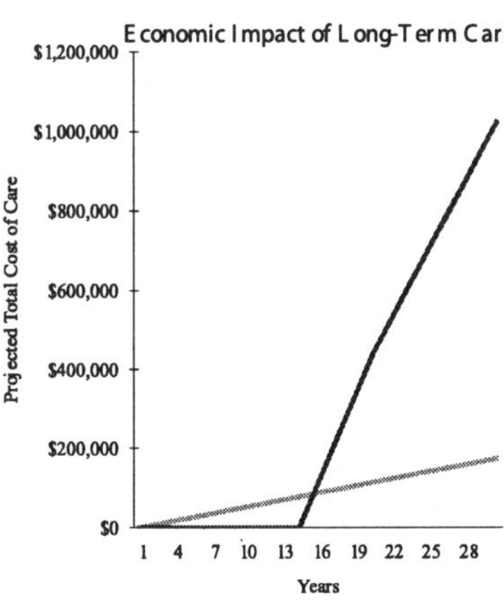

This report, and its hypothetical illustrations, are intended to form a basis for further discussion with your legal, accounting, and financial advisors. Actual future investment returns, taxes and inflation are unknown. Do not rely upon this report to predict future investment performance.

Long-Term Care Unprotected Need

This future long-term care needs chart displays the annual future amount of long-term care needed vs. your assets available. Total Long-Term Care Need is based upon average care requirements. Assets to Liquidate are your non-qualified working assets. Your Unprotected Need is $781,738 based upon these estimates.

Long-Term Care Need Calculation

Total Long-Term Care	$806,738
Assets to Liquidate:	$25,000
Unprotected Need:	$781,738

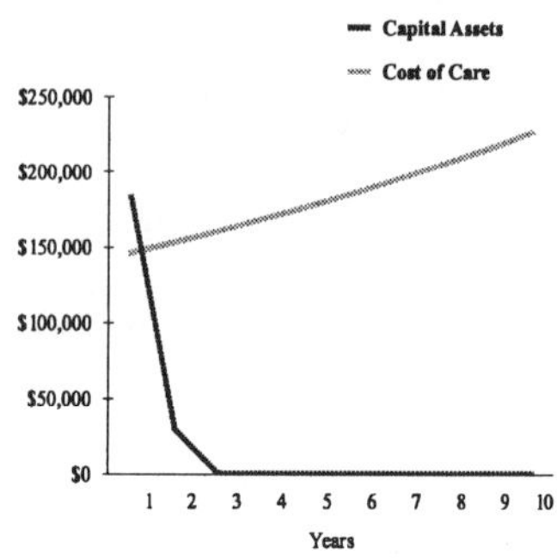

Favorable income tax treatment is available for policies meeting certain requirements. In those cases, premiums, with certain limitations, may be deducted as medical expenses for those who itemize their deductions.

Alternative Options to Long-Term Care Insurance

Self-Insurance

This alternative to purchasing LTC insurance is using your existing investments to pay for long-term care if needed. This would be appropriate if sufficient assets are available and the potential loss of those assets to heirs is acceptable. Of course this means that you are willing to liquidate your assets, and if you don't have sufficient funds, you transfer the financial burden to your loved ones. While this alternative may be more flexible, the LTC insurance would be more beneficial if the coverage is eventually needed.

Qualify for Medicaid

Medicaid was enacted to provide health care services for the impoverished. Recent legislation has made it extremely difficult for a person of modest means to qualify for Medicaid benefits by gifting or otherwise disposing of personal assets for less than fair market value.

Summary

Be aware that the potential loss of financial assets to pay for long-term care costs is due to increasing life expectancies and advances in medical treatment for the elderly. This presents a risk to your lifetime savings and financial future. LTC insurance is available at varying levels of coverage and corresponding premiums to meet these risks. LTC insurance can allow you to maintain your desired level of independence and preserve personal assets. However, premium costs will be a significant factor in your decision. Consider discussing your LTC insurance needs and options with an insurance specialist who can explain specific policy details. Fully understanding available options can help you find the best choice for you and your family's future.

Estate Planning

While a very complex topic, estate planning is a critical component of any well developed financial plan. To be effective, this planning needs to be carefully coordinated with the other areas of planning such as Insurance, Retirement, Investments, etc. The primary goal of this section is to highlight estate planning concepts, and help illustrate potential benefits of implementing basic estate planning techniques available today.

Estate Tax

Minimizing estate tax exposure is generally a primary goal of most clients. History is full of examples of estates decimated by unnecessary estate taxes and expenses. We will provide you with an analysis of your current situation and illustrate methods which may help minimize your current and future estate tax exposure. Some the basic planning techniques we will consider are the use of:

Unlimited Marital Deduction
Maximizing use of the Applicable Exclusion Amount
Unlimited Charitable Deductions
Annual Gift Exclusion
Revocable Living Trusts
Irrevocable Life Insurance Trusts

Other Financial Goals

Other financial goals to consider in your planning are:

Estate liquidity
Managing probate, administrative and other expenses
Minimizing Income Tax

Non-Financial Goals

The non-financial aspects of estate planning are just as important as the various financial goals described above. They will often be of a very personal nature and should be customized to fit into your overall plan. Generally, this can be accomplished by discussing these goals noted above. We will be able to point out only general concepts in this report. However, some of the nonfinancial goals for you to consider are:

Caring for dependents or minor children
Distribution of property to heirs
Maintaining control over assets
Lifetime planning issues such as incapacity and health care powers

Summary

Protecting your estate requires careful planning. The diverse skills required to coordinate a plan might require a team approach consisting of your financial planner, attorney, insurance specialist, accountant and investment advisor. The illustrations provided here are intended as tools to help you and your team make informed decisions. In addition, your situation will most likely change with time. Therefore, you will need to monitor your estate planning situation periodically and make amendments as required.

This report is a hypothetical illustration and does not constitute legal or tax advice. You should always obtain legal counsel and professional tax advice before taking action affecting your estate planning.

Your Current Situation

The illustrations in this report are based on information that you provided. Before reviewing the estate illustrations or investigating any of the alternatives that follow, please verify the following data and assumptions for accuracy and completeness.

Basic Data

	John	Mary
Age	48	46
Age at Death for this Illustration	48	46

General Assumptions

Administrative & probate expenses as a percentage of estate assets:	4.00%
Estimated final expenses:	$7,500

Existing Estate Planning

	John	Mary
Will	No	No
Revocable Living Trust	No	No
Marital Trust Provisions	No	No
Credit Shelter Trust Provisions	No	No
QTIP Trust Provisions	No	No
Generation Skip Trust Provisions	No	No
Irrevocable Life Insurance Trust	No	No
Durable General Power of Attorney	No	No
Durable Health Care Power of Attorney	No	No
Living Will	No	No
Existing percentage of Estate in Living Trust	0%	0%

Previous Gifting Detail

	John	Mary
Previous Taxable Gifts	$0	$0
Previous Gift Taxes Paid	$0	$0

Current Estate Summary

- John's gross estate consists of $504,500 and Mary's consists of $188,500.
- Potential federal estate taxes currently range from $0 to $0.
- Administrative, probate, and final expenses could total from $55,146 to $67,281.
- Additional planning could save up to $48,817 in estate taxes and other costs.

This report, and its hypothetical illustrations, are intended to form a basis for further discussion with your legal, accounting, and financial advisors. Actual future investment returns, taxes and inflation are unknown. Do not rely upon this report to predict future investment performance.

Estate Net Worth Statement

John and Mary Sample

ASSETS	John	Mary	Joint/ Community	Total
Savings and Investments				
Money market accounts/funds			$20,000	$20,000
Annuities	30,000			30,000
Municipal bonds and funds			10,000	10,000
Stock mutual funds			5,000	5,000
	$30,000	$0	$35,000	$65,000
Retirement Accounts				
Qualified Plans-John	$100,000			$100,000
IRA Assets-Mary		14,000		14,000
Roth IRA Assets-John	2,000			2,000
Roth IRA Assets-Mary		2,000		2,000
	$102,000	$16,000	$0	$118,000
Other Assets				
Residence			$200,000	$200,000
Personal property			20,000	20,000
Auto			30,000	30,000
	$0	$0	$250,000	$250,000
TOTAL ASSETS	$132,000	$16,000	$285,000	$433,000
LIABILITIES				
Residence mortgage			$120,000	$120,000
Auto Loans			15,000	15,000
Credit Cards			5,000	5,000
TOTAL LIABILITIES	$0	$0	$140,000	$140,000
NET WORTH	$132,000	$16,000	$145,000	$293,000
ADJUSTMENTS				
Life insurance in estate	$300,000	$100,000		
Estate share of joint property	72,500	72,500		
ESTATE NET WORTH	$504,500	$188,500		

This report, and its hypothetical illustrations, are intended to form a basis for further discussion with your legal, accounting, and financial advisors. Actual future investment returns, taxes and inflation are unknown. Do not rely upon this report to predict future investment performance.

Personalized Financial Plan John and Mary Sample

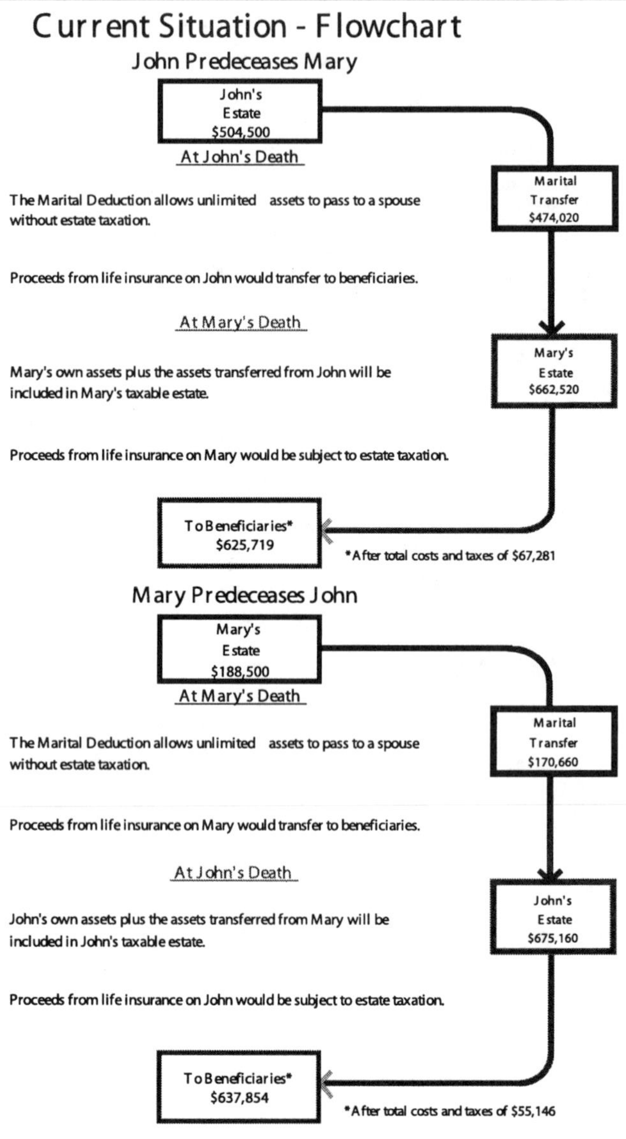

March 15, 2005 This report, and its hypothetical illustrations, are intended to form a basis for further discussion with your legal, accounting, and financial advisors. Actual future investment returns, taxes and inflation are unknown. Do not rely upon this report to predict future investment performance. Page 35 of 41

Current Situation - Estimate

John Predeceases Mary

Estate	John's Death	Mary's Death
Separate property	$30,000	$0
50% of jointly owned & community property	$142,500	$142,500
Retirement accounts	102,000	16,000
Life Insurance	300,000	100,000
Debt	(70,000)	(70,000)
Marital Transfer		474,020
	$504,500	$662,520
Deductions and Expenses		
Marital Transfer	($474,020)	
Administrative, Probate and Final expenses	(30,480)	(36,801)
	($504,500)	($36,801)
Federal Taxable Estate	$0	$625,719
Federal Estate Tax		
Federal Estate Tax	($0)	($202,316)
Applicable Credit Amount	0	202,316
Federal Estate Tax	$0	$0

Mary Predeceases John

Estate	Mary's Death	John's Death
Separate property	$0	$30,000
50% of jointly owned & community property	142,500	142,500
Retirement accounts	16,000	102,000
Life Insurance	100,000	300,000
Debt	(70,000)	(70,000)
Marital Transfer		170,660
	$188,500	$675,160
Deductions and Expenses		
Marital Transfer	($170,660)	
Administrative, Probate & Final expenses	(17,840)	(37,306)
	($188,500)	($37,306)
Federal Taxable Estate	$0	$637,854
Federal Estate Tax		
Federal Estate Tax	$0	($206,806)
Applicable Credit Amount	0	206,806
Federal Estate Tax	$0	$0

Your Alternate Estate Planning Structure

Summary of Alternative Estate Results

This report reviews and compares the cumulative impact of some potential estate planning alternatives upon your estate. The Alternative Flowchart diagram which follows this page helps illustrate how the improved estate structure reduces the amount of your estate exposed to estate taxes. In your specific case, you may be able to reduce your estate costs and taxes by up to 72%. These savings directly translate into additional assets available for beneficiaries.

Currently, your combined total estate is estimated to be $693,000. Using estimated estate settlement costs of $67,281, you would pass approximately $625,719 to your beneficiaries.

With proper implementation of potential alternative estate structures, your current estimated estate settlement costs may be reduced to approximately $18,464. This would allow you to save $48,817 in taxes and expenses, transferring $674,536 to your beneficiaries.

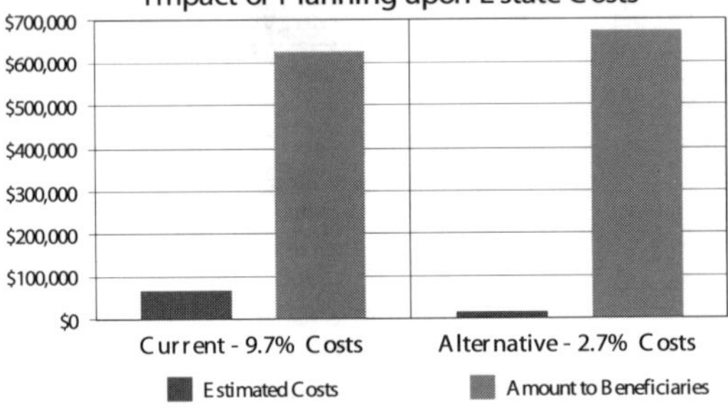

Alternative Wills and Trusts

By implementing potential alternative estate strategies, you may significantly increase the assets passing to your beneficiaries at death and reduce your estimated estate settlement costs.

Your current estate documents:

- None

Suggested additional/alternative estate documents:

- A Will for each spouse if necessary
- Revised asset ownership to balance property if necessary
- A Revocable Living Trust for each spouse
- Fund the Revocable Living Trusts
- Credit Shelter Trust provisions
- Marital Trust provisions
- Irrevocable Life Insurance Trusts
- Durable General Powers of Attorney
- Durable Health Care Powers of Attorney
- Living Wills

This report, and its hypothetical illustrations, are intended to form a basis for further discussion with your legal, accounting, and financial advisors. Actual future investment returns, taxes and inflation are unknown. Do not rely upon this report to predict future investment performance.

Alternative Situation - Flowchart

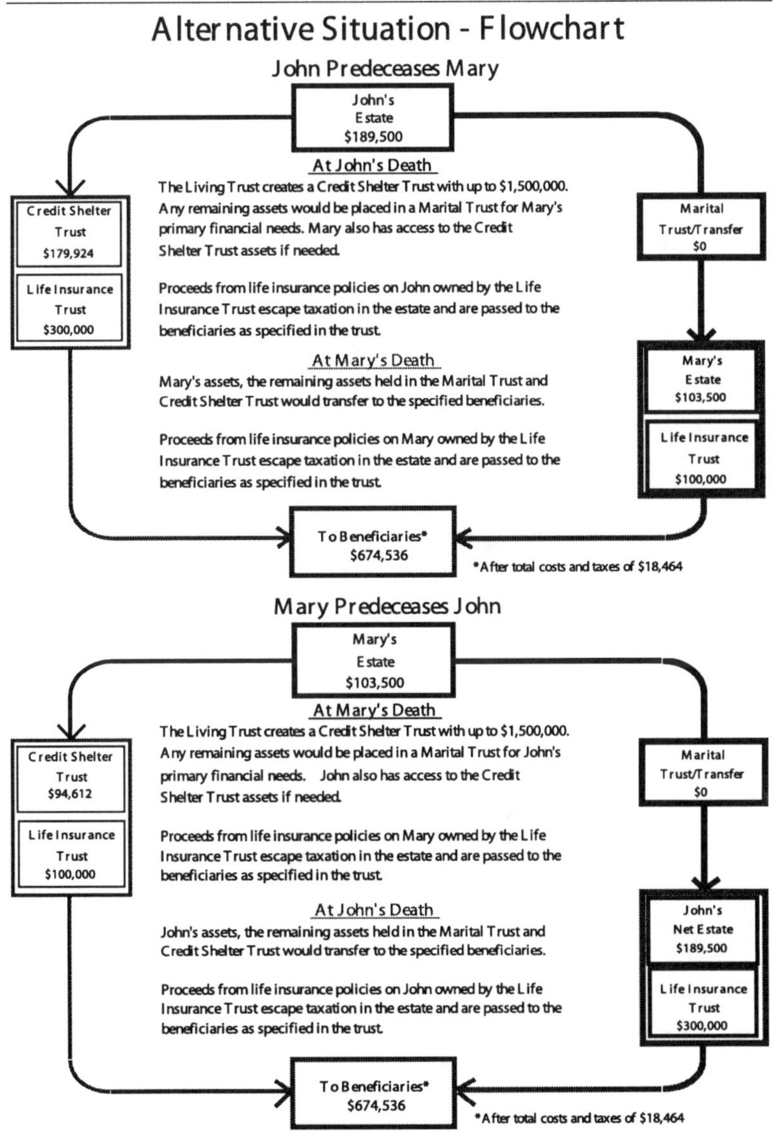

This report, and its hypothetical illustrations, are intended to form a basis for further discussion with your legal, accounting, and financial advisors. Actual future investment returns, taxes and inflation are unknown. Do not rely upon this report to predict future investment performance.

Alternative Situation - Estimate

John Predeceases Mary

	John's Death	Mary's Death
Estate		
Separate property (assets balanced)	$157,500	$157,500
Retirement accounts	102,000	16,000
Life Insurance	0	0
Debt	(70,000)	(70,000)
Marital Transfer		0
	$189,500	$103,500
Deductions and Expenses		
Marital Transfer	0	
Administrative, Probate & Final expenses	(9,576)	(8,888)
	($9,576)	($8,888)
Federal Taxable Estate	$179,924	$94,612
Federal Estate Tax		
Federal Estate Tax	($48,376)	($22,291)
Applicable Credit Amount	48,376	22,291
Federal Estate Tax	$0	$0

Mary Predeceases John

	Mary's Death	John's Death
Estate		
Separate property (assets balanced)	$157,500	$157,500
Retirement accounts	16,000	102,000
Life Insurance	0	0
Debt	(70,000)	(70,000)
Marital Transfer		0
	$103,500	$189,500
Deductions and Expenses		
Marital Transfer	0	
Administrative, Probate & Final expenses	(8,888)	(9,576)
	($8,888)	($9,576)
Federal Taxable Estate	$94,612	$179,924
Federal Estate Tax		
Federal Estate Tax	($22,291)	($48,376)
Applicable Credit Amount	22,291	48,376
Federal Estate Tax	$0	$0

Estate Tax Estimate

EGTRRA 2001

In June 2001, The Economic Growth and Tax Relief Reconciliation Act of 2001 was signed into law. One feature of the new law is to completely phase out estate taxes by 2010. This will be done by increasing estate tax exemptions and decreasing estate tax rates each year. In 2010, inherited property will no longer receive a step-up in basis as is done now, exposing those assets to potentially large capital gains when sold. In addition, Gift Tax rules have been changed. Congress must decide by 2011 if these changes will be permanent or revert back to previous law. We have shown your estate tax exposure in 2011 in terms of the previous law.

An Estimate of Your Estate Tax Exposure Using Suggested Planning

We have taken information provided about your current estate net worth to estimate your estate tax exposure under the new law over the next several years. We make some general assumptions regarding the growth of assets. Also, as previously suggested in this analysis, we assume that each individual has funded a credit shelter trust utilizing the applicable exclusion amounts available to them (currently $1,500,000 per person in 2005). We also assume that any life insurance benefits are kept out of the taxable estate. The graph below shows your estimated estate tax exposure (red) and your estate remainder after taxes (green) at each year end. Keep in mind that the status of estate tax law is uncertain beyond year 2010.

Estimated Estate Growth vs. Federal Estate Tax

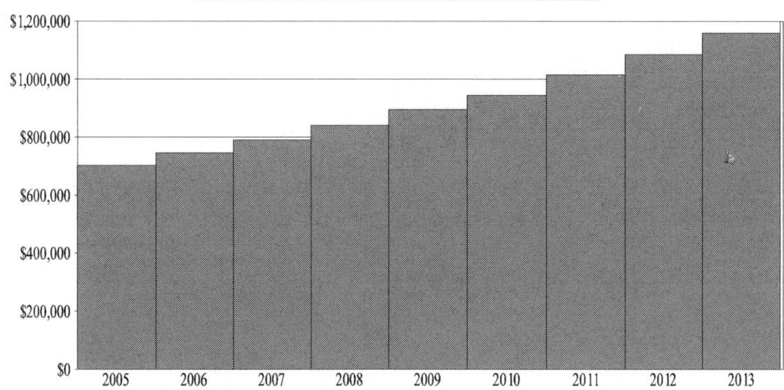

Year End	Retirement Capital	Other Assets	Debts & Expenses	Adjustments*	Estate Tax Base	Exclusion Amounts	Estimated Estate Tax
2005	$214,593	$650,000	($161,357)	$0	$703,236	$3,000,000	$0
2006	249,359	657,500	(161,695)	0	745,164	4,000,000	0
2007	287,585	665,225	(162,062)	0	790,748	4,000,000	0
2008	329,585	673,182	(162,462)	0	840,304	4,000,000	0
2009	375,701	681,377	(162,897)	0	894,181	7,000,000	0
2010	426,301	689,819	(171,186)	0	944,933	0	0
2011	481,788	698,513	(164,156)	0	1,016,145	2,000,000	0
2012	542,601	707,468	(165,210)	0	1,084,859	2,000,000	0
2013	609,218	716,693	(166,355)	0	1,159,555	2,000,000	0
2014	655,183	726,193	(167,171)	0	1,214,205	2,000,000	0

*Adjustments include charitable deductions or previous taxable gifts that have been included in your estate plan analysis.

Education Funding Illustration

John and Mary Sample

Assuming an inflation rate of 6%, the total estimated cost of education will be $176,820.

If you can invest your education funds at 6%* after taxes you may ...

-Make a single deposit now in the amount of ...	$99,998
-Make level annual payments in the amount of...	$11,962
-Make level monthly payments in the amount of...	$997

* This hypothetical rate of return is for illustrative purposes and does not represent a particular investment.

Student Name	Starting year	Number of years	Per year in today's $	Total cost at 6% inf.	Current college funds saved	529 Plan	One time deposit	Annual deposits
Janie	2009	4	$15,000	$78,153	$20,000	No	$39,999	$6,760
John	2013	4	15,000	98,667			59,999	7,177
				$176,820	$20,000		$99,998	$13,937**

The following schedule demonstrates the option of making level annual payments until the last year of education expenses. Any current funds saved will be utilized as educational expenses are incurred.

Annual Breakdown of Educational Funding

Year	Additions to fund	Paid to school from fund	Ending Balance at 6%*
2006	$11,962		$33,879
2007	11,962		48,591
2008	11,962		64,186
2009	11,962	17,865	61,779
2010	11,962	18,937	58,092
2011	11,962	20,073	52,980
2012	11,962	21,278	46,283
2013	11,962	22,554	37,832
2014	11,962	23,908	27,438
2015	11,962	25,342	14,901
2016	11,962	26,863	0

** Annual deposit total shown may be higher than the level payment amount, but decreases as each student graduates.

This report, and its hypothetical illustrations, are intended to form a basis for further discussion with your legal, accounting, and financial advisors. Actual future investment returns, taxes and inflation are unknown. Do not rely upon this report to predict future investment performance.